Bombs Away

*A B-17 Pilot's 'Small'
Part in a Big War*

Hans P. Smith

Bombs Away: A B-17 Pilot's 'Small' Part in a Big War,
by Hans P. Smith

©Copyright 2024 by Hans P. Smith. All rights reserved.

No part of this book may be reproduced in any written, electronic, recording, or photocopying without written permission of the author, with the exception of quotations used for critical articles or reviews where permission is specifically given by the author.

Although every precaution has been taken to verify the accuracy of the information contained herein, the author assumes no responsibility for any errors or omissions. No liability is assumed for damages that may result from the use of information contained within.

Cover design by Hans P. Smith.

Books may be purchased wherever books are sold, or by contacting the author at:
hanssmith72@hotmail.com

ISBN: 979-8-9920733-0-0 (soft cover)
979-8-9920733-1-7 (eBook)

Dedication

This work is dedicated to my great-uncle Herbert Small, pilot and co-pilot of B-17 Flying Fortresses during World War II, flying and fighting out of Grafton-Underwood Airbase in England, as well as to all the men of the 384th Bombardment Group with whom he served.

It is also dedicated to the many brave men and women of the American military, especially of the World War II generation, who served their country with such bravery and distinction. Without their sacrifices, the world would be a very different place today.

It is lastly dedicated to all of the men who didn't come home and the brave men and women of the occupied countries who helped so many men of the 384th Bombardment Group, like Kenneth Hougard, evade capture and return home, at great personal risk to themselves.

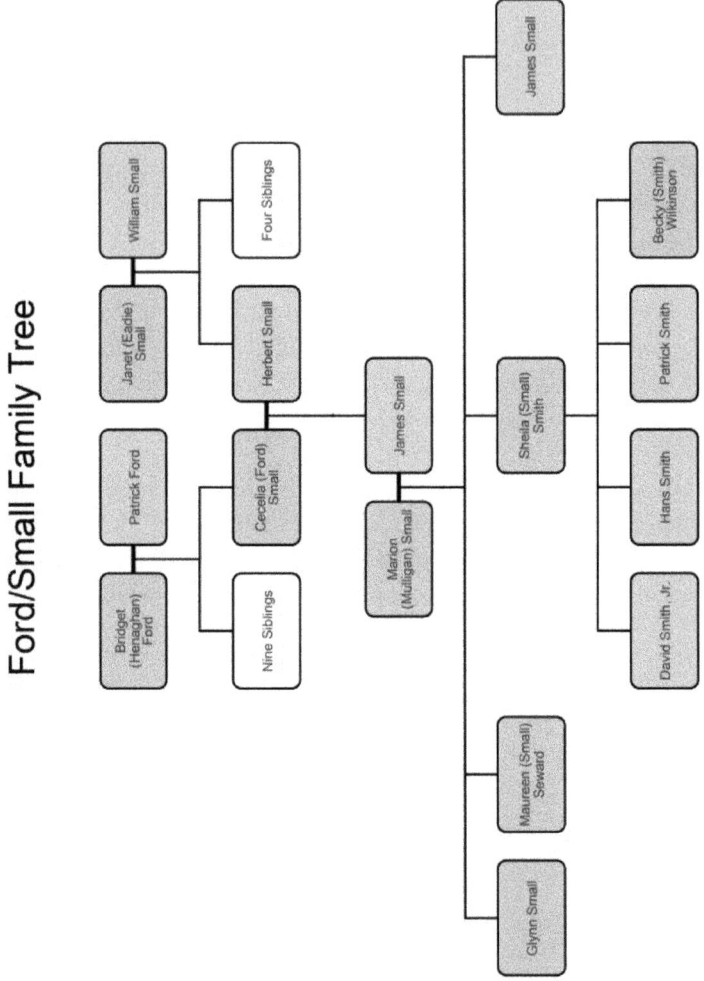

Table of Contents

Introduction 1
Sheffield 5
Training 23
Grafton-Underwood Airbase 41
The Flying Fortress 69
The Crew 95
1943 Missions 115
1944 Missions 139
Final Missions 163
POWs 189
Evade and Escape 209
Conclusion 225
Bibliography 233
Acknowledgements and Thanks 238
Index 240

Introduction

A recent vacation that my wife and I took to France is probably as close as I'll ever get to going on a pilgrimage, even though I didn't think of it as such until some weeks afterwards. The goal was to find a family member that I had never met but had heard about all of my life. He had died twenty-eight years before I was born, seven years before my mother was born and only twenty-three and a half years into his life. His memory had been kept alive in my family's collective memory and by way of their stories, always spoken with reverence.

I wasn't sure what I expected to find or learn from the experience, but it felt like something I needed to do. It was part of a larger trip, so it wasn't our sole focus, but it was foremost in my mind. When family members learned about where we were going on the trip, they began to send me information about my great-uncle, which only piqued my curiosity further. The more I learned, the more eager I was for the trip to begin!

Our vacation plans included a visit to the American Cemetery in Normandy, which is the final resting place for 9,386 of our military men who lost their lives in the Normandy region during World War II. My great-uncle Herbert W. Small is among them.

Bombs Away

The cemetery is located near the small French coastal village of Colleville-sur-Mer, which was a pivotal location in the battle for Omaha Beach in June of 1944. It is the famous cemetery that is prominently featured in the film *Saving Private Ryan* and is seen regularly on television around the anniversary of D-Day each year. It is a place that I have wanted to visit for a very long time, and I was finally going to see it.

When we first arrived at the cemetery, we were struck by its beauty and serenity. A few hundred yards from Omaha Beach, the one-time site of chaotic battle is now dominated by peace and tranquility. We walked and admired the beautifully manicured grounds, but soon noticed that visitors were required to stay on the walkways and not allowed amongst the graves. We were immediately disheartened, feeling like the visit would seem a letdown if we weren't able to see his grave up close.

It occurred to me as we walked that hundreds of men had fought and died on and near the very ground we now walked upon. The soil is literally mixed with the blood and tears and shattered dreams of so many of our brave young men. We were on hallowed ground.

We eventually found a cemetery guide and asked if it would be possible to see an individual grave. What happened next was truly amazing and humbling… and something I'll never forget.

I really didn't think we would be allowed to see it…to actually walk amongst the graves. I was expecting a polite, "No, monsieur. Ce n'est pas permis." ("It's not allowed.") We would have respected their policy but would have been terribly disappointed. Instead, the guide asked, in French-accented English, "You are family?" I replied, "Oui," and things started to happen.

Orders were given to a young man named "Theo," who disappeared into a service area and returned with two small flags — American and French — and a small container of sand, which we soon learned was from Omaha Beach itself.

Theo escorted us to the gravesite, where he proceeded to place the small flags — like those I waved as a boy at my hometown Memorial Day parades — on either side of the immaculate white marble cross. He

Introduction

then instructed me to smear a handful of the sand across the lettering on the marker, which I didn't understand at first. I soon realized that the sand fills in the engraving and makes the letters stand out from the white marble in photographs. It eventually washes out with the wind and rain and becomes part of the cemetery itself, which seems fitting.

Once the sand was in place, we stood back to take pictures. As we did — Spielberg himself could not have scripted this any better — "Taps" began to play from somewhere else in the cemetery, likely part of some other ceremony in progress. This 51-year-old man who is two generations removed from a great-uncle he never knew…was driven to tears…for reasons I only partially understood. That was the day my great-uncle became a real person to me, and my personal journey to discover who he was began.

What the sand revealed was:

HERBERT W. SMALL
1 LT 544 BOMB SQ 384 BOMB GP (H)
MASSACHUSETTS APR 27 1944

This is his story.

Bombs Away

1st Lt. Herbert W. Small's grave at the American Cemetery in Normandy, May 2023.

Sheffield

1

This story starts where every good story starts…at the beginning. And the beginning of Herbert Small's story is in Sheffield, Massachusetts, in a small, white house on Salisbury Road, a couple of miles southwest of the center of town. The house originally belonged to his grandfather, and was passed through the generations, still in his (my) family until only recently.

Herbert William Small was born on December 23, 1920 to Herbert (the elder) and Cecelia (Ford) Small in the small Western Massachusetts town of Sheffield, the second of five children born to first-generation Scottish and Irish immigrants. His grandparents on his father's side — William Small and Janet (Eadie) Small — lived in Scotland and never immigrated to America. His grandparents on his mother's side — Patrick Ford and Bridget Henaghan — were born in Ireland but immigrated to the United States in their young adult years sometime between 1860 and 1870. Son of William and Janet Small, Herbert W. Small (the elder) was born in Alva, Scotland, but moved to America as a young man, likely drawn by the prospect of work and a better life than was available in the then impoverished Scotland.

Patrick Ford was a farmer who could not read or write, but he ran his farm on Salisbury Road in Sheffield and provided for his wife and ten children, living in a roughly 1,200 square-foot home that still stands today. It is the same home in which I spent the first two years of my life, when my young parents were waiting to begin construction on their own home, to be situated a couple hundred yards away on a piece of land that was once part of the Ford farm. Sharing that same little home, however briefly and two generations apart, was the first tangible connection I found with my great-uncle.

> [I realized very quickly as I dove into the research for this story that I had a tremendous amount of shared experience with my great-uncle Herb. I spent much of my own childhood living in his footsteps. As a small child, I slept in the same bedroom, ate in the same kitchen, bathed in the same bathtub and sat on the same small porch. As an older child, I played in the same yard, attended the same school and borrowed books from the same library...I even attended the same church.]

Life for that first generation of newly arrived Fords was very hard in a time of limited conveniences and grueling manual labor, and no doubt the children were an integral part of the daily chores and farm work. According to the U. S. National Census of 1870, the family owned $400 worth of personal property and their farm was valued at roughly $1,800. They were far from well-off, with the equivalent values in today's dollars being roughly $38,000 and $170,000, though that's only an inflation estimate and not a value of what the actual real estate would be worth today. The land has been divided among other family members and descendants over the decades and generations.

Their day-to-day life consisted of farm chores, cooking, making and mending clothes and taking care of the smaller children. The chil-

Sheffield

The William & Janet (Eadie) Small family in Alva, Scotland, circa 1894. Young Herbert Small (the elder) is the handsome chap seated with his father.
(Photo courtesy of the Small family.)

dren attended school and shared in many of the chores as soon as they were old enough. For Patrick Ford and his sons, days were started early and mostly spent outside. The land was very fertile in Berkshire County — the westernmost county in Massachusetts — and still is today. However, that part of New England is also known for "growing stones." Winter ice and frosts push a seemingly endless supply of rocks and stones up through the soil into fields, almost as if someone had sown pebbles the previous fall, with a spring harvest in mind. This meant that plowing fields — in those days with horses, mules and good old fashioned manual labor — was very difficult and often frustrating work, with broken plows and aching backs commonplace. Farming was not an easy trade in those days, nor is it today.

But there was quiet family time, as well, in the evenings especially. And church on Sundays, of course. If the kids were anything like we were three generations later, their mothers had to holler at them around dusk to get them to come in from playing late into the evening. In the

Bombs Away

Heavy snow at the Small family house on Salisbury Road.

winters, which are often cold and harsh in the Berkshires, evenings were spent around the potbellied stove that was still part of the house almost a century later when my parents with two young sons briefly lived there. Around the fire, there was knitting, sewing, books, stories, games and homework to keep them company on the long, cold nights.

On those cold winter nights, each family member was likely to have taken a hot soapstone — a piece of very dense, almost metallic stone about the size of a thin hardcover book — from atop the woodstove and wrapped it in a bath towel or blanket to place at the foot of their beds under the covers. The soapstones would give off enough heat to keep each bed's occupant warm and cozy through the night. It was something we still did in our own home several decades later.

Sheffield, Massachusetts was a very small agricultural town in those days, with a population of about 2,200 at the turn of the twentieth century. It is still small today, with only 3,327 residents as of the 2020

Sheffield

Census. Nestled in the southwest corner of Massachusetts, the town is more or less bisected by the north/south running Housatonic River, which flows through the lower half of Berkshire County, winding its way into Connecticut, where it eventually makes its way to the Long Island Sound.

Guarded to the west by the imposing and majestic Mount Everett and to the east by smaller but still formidable hills, Sheffield sits in the Housatonic River Valley, the river having helped provide much of the rich soil for farming throughout its history. Sheffield was the first town incorporated in what is now Berkshire County, established on June 22, 1733, purchased from the Konkapot Indian tribe native to the area. The town is bordered to the north by Great Barrington, which was originally the Northern Parish of Sheffield, to the west by Mount Washington, to the east by New Marlborough and to the south by Canaan, Connecticut. It is also divided nearly into equal parts by what was once the Housatonic Railroad, running north and south through Berkshire County. As a young man not long out of high school in the seventies, my father became an engineer for the railroad company Conrail, and often drove trains on that line, headed for various towns throughout Connecticut and New York.

Sheffield had a variety of industries at the turn of the 20th century, including sawmills, grist mills, blacksmiths, tanneries, marble quarries and farms. There were at least four churches, up to fourteen schoolhouses, dairies and even trade in tobacco, tin- and stone-wares. There were a couple of small-town doctors and even a cheese factory, which stood about three quarters of a mile east of where Our Lady of the Valley Catholic Church stands today on Maple Avenue.

Many of the buildings and homes from Sheffield's early history are still there today, and they help to preserve a beautiful example of a classic New England Colonial town. Maps of the town from around the turn of the twentieth century show the locations of each individual home, business, church and school that existed at the time of the map's printing. Located on one such map from 1904 is the home of Patrick Ford and his family on Salisbury Road.

Bombs Away

The Ford Children — six boys, John, Frank, Thomas, Patrick, Edward and James -- and four girls, Mary, Ellen, Nora and Cecelia — were spread over sixteen years, with the eldest Thomas born in 1870 and Cecelia the youngest born in 1886. Mary, the first-born girl born in 1872 died in 1885 at the young age of thirteen, of causes unknown to me. Her death was soon followed the next April by the birth of the last of Ford children, Cecelia, who bore Mary's name as her middle name, no doubt in tribute to the lost sister she never knew.

[I'm going to go ahead and give you fair warning early on that the Irish and Scottish in those times (and still today, let's be honest) had the very endearing yet endlessly confusing practice of re-using the same first names over and over again! Not only was my Great-Uncle Herb's father also named Herbert, his mother Cecelia shared her name with her daughter Cecelia. You don't have to look far in an Irish family tree to find plenty of people named Ann, Mary, Patrick, James, William, Herbert, Peter and Cecelia, to name a few. And if it's not the first name, it's likely to be the middle name. You know what name you don't find in an Irish or Scottish family tree? HANS!!. But I digress...that's a story for a beer not a book. Bear with me through the name thing and you'll survive this chapter no worse for the wear.]

Herbert Small (the elder) spent some time in the Marines between 1910 and 1914, from age twenty-one to twenty-five, but fortunately he was honorably discharged before he could be called to service in World War I. Two years later, he married Cecelia Ford, the youngest of the Ford children in 1916 (he was twenty-seven and she was twenty-four), and it wasn't long before they started their own family. I don't know how they came to meet or know one another, despite efforts to find

Sheffield

Herbert Small (the elder) and Cecelia Ford Small. Circa 1918
(Courtesy of the Small family.)

their history.

The first of the Herbert and Cecelia Small children — young Herbert's older brother James (Jim) — was born on April 22, 1918, and two and a half years later, Herb arrived on December 23, 1920. Several years later, on April 22 again (1927), James received a very special birthday present when his first little sister Mary was born. (This wasn't the only such happy coincidence in our family regarding birthdays; I happened to have been born on my father's birthday, as well.)

The final addition to the no-longer-small Small family came a little more than two years later, when twin girls Ann and Cecelia (Cece) were welcomed on September 22, 1928. Proud parents Herbert and Cecelia Small lived in the Ford family home in Sheffield with their growing family for the first fifteen years or so of their marriage, with all five children being born while living there, until about 1931.

During that time, the kids' Uncle Tommy Ford, the eldest of the Ford children, also lived with them. He had been struck blind years before when he was kicked in the head by an ordinarily docile plow-horse.

Bombs Away

The Small family — Mother Cecelia "Nanny" Small, Father Herbert Small, Jim and Herb, and one of the Ford uncles. Cece, Mary and Ann in front. Circa 1932 (Courtesy of the Small family.)

He learned to cope well with the injury and even went on to craft a set of specialized checkers, carving both round and square pieces from wood, and making a special notch on the opposite side to denote when a player would get "kinged." He lived until age sixty-one and died in 1931. At the time of his death, while his body lay for viewing in the family living room, the barn somehow caught fire. Though the barn was destroyed, the fire was thankfully kept from spreading to the house.

The barn was never rebuilt, but there were still several other farm outbuildings in operation, including a chicken coop and a multi-purpose pole barn where equipment could be stored. On the spot of the old barn, since the 1970s, stands the current and longtime home of one of the Small's nieces, Maureen (Small) Seward, my aunt and Godmother. That spot would hold special significance for the next generation of Smalls, to be described a little later in this chapter.

The Small (and small) home would have been nearly busting at

Sheffield

the seams, with three adults, two teen boys, and three young girls all sharing the space, but that was nothing new for the home, having previously housed the Fords and their ten children. The Small children shared the small bedrooms and even beds, at times. With that many people in the house, there was little room for luxury or privacy. At one point, a mattress was moved into a hallway temporarily to allow for more room, according to my ninety-six-year-old Aunt Mary, the last surviving of the Small children. She recently told me, before her passing, "We didn't know any different and didn't worry about much. That's just how it was, and we didn't know that there was any other way. It was just normal life

The Small children in Sheffield, circa 1932 - Herb and Jim (L-to-R), the twins Ann and Cece in front, and Mary in the middle. Circa 1930
(Courtesy of the Small family.)

to us. We didn't complain." That mindset is certainly a rarity today.

For a time, Herbert the elder owned and operated a small electrician's shop in the building that would eventually become The Sheffield Pub, on the corner of Route 7 and Miller Avenue, and across the street from the Sheffield Inn, which is no longer there. The family lived there for a short time, between 1931 and 1933, in the apartment above the store, until they moved for a little while to a home just east of the center of town, presumably to have more space for their growing family.

Young Herb was close with his siblings, as often was the case in a time when family was critically important and there weren't distractions like television or the internet to take up all of their time. His younger sisters were particularly important to him, as with any good big brother, and their affection for each other was noted in pictures and various correspondence through the years. Herb has been described by his sisters as being very well-liked, with no one having a bad word to say about him.

One story of their childhood features Herb in his mid-teens getting a lesson in stubborn determination from his kid sister Cece, one of the twin girls born last in the family.

During the time when the family was living in the small house to the east of the center of Sheffield around 1935, one winter day, one of their father's electrical customers paid his bill with a check, which had been picked up by 14-year-old Herb at the Sheffield Post Office. During the walk home along Maple Avenue — past Our Lady of the Valley Catholic Church and across the Housatonic River by way of what was at the time reputedly one of the oldest covered bridges in Massachusetts — Herb dropped the check somewhere. He only discovered it was missing when he arrived home.

It was a very important check that the family very much needed, so he and Cece — his strong-willed kid sister of about six or seven who insisted on coming along to help — ventured back out into the cold, snowy day in search of the lost check. They retraced Herb's steps, found the check, and the day was saved, but it must have been a very stressful moment for everyone. The loss of even a single coveted paycheck

Sheffield

Herb and the girls, Cece, Mary and Ann, plus a buddy named Wally, heading to the swimming hole. Circa 1932

in those days could have meant disaster for a family of seven trying to make ends meet during the Depression.

Eventually, around 1936, the Small family moved back into the Ford farm home on Salisbury Road, where they would live from that point forward. 1936 was also the year in which their father Herbert passed away, so it would prove to be a very challenging time for the family. The farm was much smaller than it had been in the earlier days and was no longer the full working farm that it had once been. While they had been living elsewhere, other members of the Ford family had occupied the home.

In their free time, the kids would sometimes swim in the nearby Schenob Brook, which ran directly behind their property, and was known as "the Swimming Hole," to them and their friends. Several photos from that time show a happy and healthy family enjoying simple small-town life, despite the struggles the country was experiencing. I spent many hours fishing in that same brook as a child, though we rarely swam in it because the banks were largely overgrown by my time, and the brook itself was very muddy on the bottom, and rumored to have

Bombs Away

quick-sand, though I wonder now if that was just a story the grown-ups told us kids to keep us away from the brook.

Hours were spent reading, playing outside, making up games and doing chores around the house. Herb liked to fish and hunt, but older brother Jim was not so keen on such activities, according to his sister Cece, still alive as of the early stages of writing this book. They were of very different temperaments, and enjoyed different activities, she told me. One passion the two brothers did share was baseball. They both played baseball for the local Sheffield AA, team, which I believe stood for the Sheffield "Athletic Association." Herb's younger sister Mary, the oldest of the girls, enjoyed helping her mother around the kitchen, and eagerly learned her incredible cooking and baking skills that are still in

Jim and Herb in their Sheffield A.A. baseball uniform, circa 1936.
(Courtesy of the Small family.)

Sheffield

use today as of this writing, some ninety years later. Young Mary would follow her mother around the kitchen, eventually learning to cook full meals for the family when her mother had occasional health issues.

Life wasn't easy in Sheffield. People worked hard for what they had, and when the Great Depression came, times were even harder. Young Herb would have only been nine or ten years old at the start of the Depression, and it certainly would have made a strong impression on a child of that age at the time. In the days long before television or even the common usage of the telephone and radio, the bonds of family were very strong, often to a degree that is hard to fathom in our current culture.

Certainly the Great Depression affected small-town Sheffield in similar ways as the rest of the country, but there's no indication that the family suffered in any greater proportion than the average American family. They ran a smaller version of the Ford farm, and it's likely that the multiple sources of food made a difference in day-to-day life. Fresh milk, eggs and meat, along with vegetables that could be eaten fresh, cooked or canned and pickled to be saved for later certainly helped to get them through the lean months. No doubt the abundance of firewood from the woods nearby gave them a large supply to feed the potbellied stove and fend off the very cold New England winters.

Jim and Herb, from all accounts, were good big brothers to their three little sisters, and speaking from experience, having little sisters is one of the best ways to ingrain a protective instinct in a young man. It is likely that this helped both Jim and Herb develop the sense of duty and protection early in life, and that it would have contributed to their desire to volunteer for military service when the war in Europe and the Pacific was in its early days.

Herb and Jim attended Sheffield area elementary and grammar schools, and eventually Sheffield High School, which was still relatively new at the time. It had been built to consolidate the disparate system of one-room schoolhouses that were scattered throughout the town. At one point, there were fourteen different schoolhouses in Sheffield, mostly located in the small villages like Ashley Falls, which must have made for a very chaotic educational experience.

Jim graduated from Sheffield High School in 1936, around the time his father passed away. Being the oldest child and now the man of the house, Jim shouldered a good portion of the burden, working electrical jobs in Pittsfield — about thirty miles to the north of Sheffield — and other towns in Berkshire County in order to earn money to help support the family. In those days, it would not have been feasible to commute daily to work thirty or forty miles away from home, so young Jim, not yet

Sheffield High School. The building that would eventually become Sheffield Center School and then the new Sheffield Library. Circa 1936.
(Courtesy of the family.)

out of his teens, arranged to rent a room and sometimes boarded with friends while away. He even refused to marry his girlfriend at the time because of his responsibility to his mother and four younger siblings. That alone tells us a lot about his character, dedication to his family and his responsibility as a provider.

Herb graduated from Sheffield High School two years later with the Class of 1938 and was known as a clever and hard-working student. In his younger years, he once constructed in the family home a model of a telegraph system, using the main room of the house to demonstrate how the undersea cable ran from Europe to the United States. Herb was

Sheffield

a voracious reader, and reportedly had read just about everything the small Sheffield Bushnell Sage library had to offer. He would bring home an armload of books and read into the late hours of the night. The town librarian of decades, Willard French, noticed the volume of books Herb would check out, and became dubious, so he began to subtly quiz the young man on the contents of various books, a casual question here and there. He commented later to other Small family members that he was never able to stump young Herb. Not even once.

The building that used to house Sheffield's Bushnell Sage library in those days still stands and was a regular part of my youth growing up in Sheffield, as well. I can still tell you exactly where various books were kept, including one of my childhood favorites, the entire Hardy Boys collection. Today, that building houses the Sheffield Police Department, and the library is now located where Sheffield High School and then Sheffield Center elementary school stood for many decades.

Herb was known by the nickname "Hum" to his pals (though I don't know why) and enjoyed playing basketball and baseball as a teen. His sister Cece, who had helped him on his snowy search for the missing check, near the end of her life more than eight decades later, described him as a "Very smart, good-looking, popular, kind and serious young man." She said, "Girls were practically carrying his books in school, or at least holding his jacket while he shot hoops." It was clear that she still held a lot of affection for her big brother even all those decades later.

[The fact that my ninety-something-year-old great-aunt used the term "shot hoops" still makes me smile.]

Years later after the war, when Jim -- my grandfather -- returned from the war, he followed in his father's footsteps and became an electrician, running a successful business and later becoming the Sheffield town Electrical Inspector during his semi-retired years. I have very fond memories as a child of exploring the shelves and workbenches of my grandfather's garage and workshop. The seemingly endless array and variety of knobs and wires and porcelain doohickeys were magical to a kid with a vivid imagination. They seemed like something out of an old science fiction story by H.G. Wells or Isaac Asimov.

Jim was given a few acres of land by his mother around the time he married after the war and built a home on part of what had been the old Ford farm. A generation later in the early 1970s, his daughter (my mother) Sheila Small, was also given a couple of acres of the old farmland by her father and mother, Jim and Marion (Mulligan) Small. She and my father built the home she still owns and lives in today. Her sister Maureen (Small) Seward, my aunt and Godmother, was also given a very special piece of land where the old barn used to stand before it burned. My aunt, now in her seventies, remembers a conversation with her grandmother, Cecelia — who was always known to us as "Nanny" — when she was just a young girl about how she someday wanted to build and live in a house where the old barn stood. Hearing that story from her recently made me very happy, because it's exactly what happened... and she's lived there for roughly half a century.

Decades later, yet another generation of the Small family — two of the grandsons of eldest brother Jim Small — also own homes on part of what was the old Ford farm, though that land had belonged to another farmer in the area for a few decades in between. The homes, the land and the legacy of the Fords have survived through five generations and until very recently, even the original Ford home was still in the family. Patrick and Bridget Ford and their descendants have been on that land for nearly a hundred and fifty years. That is a legacy and lineage of which they would be very proud. Their children, grandchildren, great-grandchildren, great-great-grand-children and great-great-GREAT-grandchildren have lived on -- and are still living on -- land that they originally owned as poor immigrants struggling to make a new life in a new land.

In 1942, the war called both Jim and Herb away, along with a few other young men from our family whose stories are just as interesting. They both flew on bombers; Jim as a navigator, Herb as a pilot. They both fought for their country and their loved ones. Jim came home. Herb did not.

But Herb lives on through the memories and the stories told by those who knew him, who are nearly all gone now, sadly. He lives on

Sheffield

through the memorials to his life in his hometown of Sheffield, at the site of his death near Rocheville, France and at his final resting place in the American Cemetery in Normandy. He also lives on through the words on these pages. He touched many lives, directly and indirectly, on two continents in his short time here...and he will not be forgotten.

The view of Main Street in Sheffield, circa 1950 looking north from the intersection of Berkshire School Road and Route 7, from the lawn of the old Bushnell Safe Library. (Courtesy of the Berkshire Eagle.)

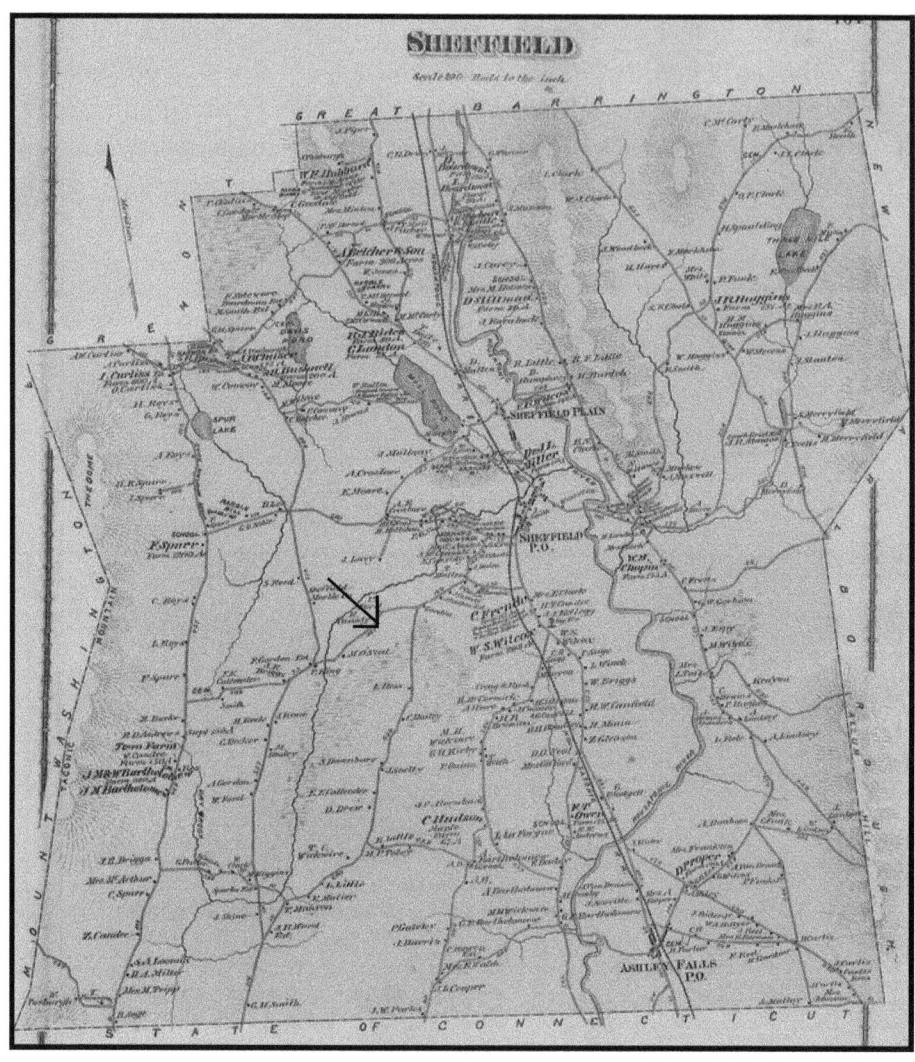

Map of Sheffield, MA, circa 1904. The Patrick Ford home can be seen slightly to the left and down from the middle. Ford farm marked by the arrow.

Phartzac

Training

2

After graduating from Sheffield High School in 1938, Herbert "Hum" Small attended the McLean Hospital Nursing School in Waverly, Massachusetts, about six miles northwest of Boston. He was away from home for much of this time, but that didn't stop his mother Cecelia from occasionally packing up the car with a picnic lunch and three little sisters and making the long, winding drive through pre-Interstate-Highway Massachusetts to see him. It's not surprising to me that he was interested in a career in nursing and medicine, having learned that his overall nature, according to those who knew him, was of a caring individual who wanted to help people.

In fact, his little sister Cece followed in his footsteps and became a nurse, working for many years at Fairview Hospital in Great Barrington, Massachusetts, the hospital where many of my family were born and treated over the years. This seems a fitting career choice for her because, for one thing, she so revered her big brother Herb, and for another, she and her twin sister Ann hold the distinction of being the first babies born in the new Maternity Ward of Fairview Hospital in September 1928. Many years later, she proudly helped deliver two other very special babies on the same day for two very special new young mothers;

her two nieces, who each delivered their first child on October 20th, 1970, another of the happy coincidences in our family; my older brother and cousin share the same exact birthday.

Herb graduated from McLean Hospital Nursing School in April of 1942 as a Registered Nurse in the Commonwealth of Massachusetts. His original plan was to go on to medical school once he completed his nursing program, but fate had other plans, as war was already raging in multiple theaters around the world. Within days of his graduation, he enlisted in the Army Air Force. Pearl Harbor had been attacked, the United States had declared war on the Empire of Japan, and patriotic young men all over the country were lining up to fight. Herb and Jim were among the first in Sheffield to volunteer for service, according to several accounts.

One of the reasons Herb related to his family for why he enlisted specifically in the Army Air Force — the precursor to the modern U.S. Air Force — was, according to his sister Cece, that he wanted to go into the war as an officer, and because "he didn't want to die face down in the mud," like might happen if he were in the infantry. Little did he know that conditions tens of thousands of feet above the mud would be no picnic either, and when the enemy flak and fighters showed up, they did not discriminate by rank. Many accounts of the air battles of B-17 Flying Fortresses, B-24 Liberators and their fighter escorts reveal that the skies over Europe and the Pacific were some of the most dangerous territory in all of the war, with the Eighth Air Force having one of the highest casualty rates of all.

Another possible reason for Herb's and Jim's desire to fly very well could have come from the romantic, adventurous aspect that aviation held at the time as still a new and growing fascination in the hearts and imaginations of young men and boys. Flying in the 1930s and 1940s was not the commonplace, mundane thing that it has become in our modern lives. Philip Kaplan and Rex A. Smith put it very well in their wonderful book, *One Last Look: A Sentimental Journey to the Eighth Force Heavy Bomber Bases of World War II in England*: "Indeed it was considered a glamorous thing to do, and of course he had wanted to fly.

Training

So had the others in the flight crews, and so had the thousands more who had applied but failed to qualify for flying duty. And they had good reason for wanting to. Most of them were born within twenty years after the Wright Brothers first flew at Kitty Hawk. While they were growing up, aviation was still an exciting new frontier, the sky was considered a habitat for heroes, and small boys dreamed of becoming fliers just as their grandfathers as boys may have dreamed of becoming railroad engineers. They were at about kindergarten age when Lindbergh flew the Atlantic, and in the following winter there was hardly a tyke in the land who did not go about with his head proudly encased in a "Lucky Lindy" helmet complete with goggles. It was a time when young boys saw Wings and other films glorifying the army pilots in World War I, then shattered their mothers' nerves by racing through the house waving toy airplanes in grubby fists and shouting, "Eeeerrrowww! Ah-ah-ah-ah! I'm Eddie Rickenbacker chasing the Red Baron!"

At the time that Jim and Herb enlisted (April of 1942), England was putting up a brave defense in the skies over their island kingdom in the Battle of Britain, to keep Hitler from conquering another of the few European nations he didn't already control and occupy. The Soviet Union, our ally at the time, but future enemy, was fighting tooth and nail against Operation Barbarossa, the Nazi's treacherous invasion of their beloved Motherland. [This was done after both countries signed the Treaty of Non-Aggression in 1939].

The United States was struggling to recover from the horrible surprise attack on Pearl Harbor and trying to find a way to push back against Japan and their massive territorial gains in the Pacific. In the early days of the war in the Pacific, the United States was trying desperately to hold back the Japanese, who seemed nearly unstoppable. There were several major battles, including the Battle of Midway, which were critical to our survival. Had they gone the other way, it could have very possibly meant defeat for the U.S. in the Pacific, and the globe could look very different today.

In August of 1942, Herb was called up to active service to begin

Bombs Away

his Primary Training at Merced, California. He said goodbye to his family and friends and traveled by bus from Berkshire County to Boston, where he departed by train from Back Bay Station, headed for the opposite coast. He traveled over three thousand miles and almost the entire length of the country in the days that followed, a long and no doubt exhausting journey. For a young man who had barely been out of the state, it had to also be both an exciting and frightening time.

The train was made up of mostly old Pullman cars, with a few dining cars and baggage cars, and the men were very tightly packed in, alternating shared bunks and spending long days and nights crammed in together. This transportation was not intended to be luxurious; there is little room for creature comforts in a time of war. It was meant to get them efficiently from one place to another so they could proceed with the task at hand.

They would have been exhausted and out of sorts by the time they arrived at their final destinations. It is likely, though I'm not certain, that Herb's route brought him through New York City down into Pennsylvania, out through Pittsburgh, central Ohio, Indianapolis and down through Saint Louis's Union Station, which was a common transit point for soldiers, sailors and airmen during the war years, both on their way to and from the war.

[Another likely small link between my great-uncle and me; I have lived in St. Louis for the last twenty-two years.]

I can imagine that this opportunity to see the country by rail would have been fascinating to a young man of Herb's nature and intelligence; eager to learn and to experience the world around him. On his trip west, he saw it from the ground…and by way of his training and eventual deployment, he saw much of it from the air, as well. I wonder if that distinction occurred to Herb as he later flew back over many of the states that he had passed through on his way to training a year or so earlier. Did there perhaps exist in the young man so fond of reading a

Training

bit of a philosopher?

As the miles rolled by, the fresh new recruits played cards, smoked, read, shot dice, wrote letters to family and sweethearts and generally killed time any way they could. Knowing the stories of his voracious reading habits, I believe my great-uncle Herb would have found a way to stuff a few good books into his duffle bags, and probably would have traded with the other soldiers when he had exhausted his own supply. Though they occupied themselves with a variety of ways to pass the time, certainly their thoughts wandered frequently to what their future held. They knew very little about what lay ahead of them, but they knew they wanted to do their part fighting for their country; they wanted to make a difference. They were fighting for their hometowns, their parents, their siblings and their friends…and they were soon to be fighting for each other, after forming some of the strongest bonds that can be formed among men.

Their thoughts undoubtedly turned to the loved ones and hometowns they had left behind, as well as to the great adventure that lay ahead of them. They came from big cities like Boston, New York and Philadelphia, smaller cities like Albany, Hartford and Utica, as well as small towns too many to name…like Sheffield. Some of these men had never ridden on a train or even driven an automobile. Many had never even left their own county or state, much less travelled all the way across the country. Leaving the United States headed for England, Northern Africa or somewhere in the Pacific must have seemed like a trip to the moon or Mars by our standards today.

There were farm boys, city boys, rich kids and poor kids. There were Italians, Irish, Germans and Latinos, just to name a few. There were guys who had graduated from college and guys who had barely made it out of high school…and those who had lied about their age and enlisted before they had even finished high school. The men were from everywhere and from all walks of life, and they mostly shared a common purpose. Most of them wanted desperately to get into the fight; they wanted to do their part and stand up for a country they loved, and avenge the vicious attack on Pearl Harbor and stand up to their enemies, Nazi Germany, Fascist Italy and the Empire of Japan. Men who were deemed physically unfit for duty — 4F, in the military parlance of the day — were often so distraught that suicide among them was not uncommon. Of those who were fit for duty (1A), some would go on to fight in the infantry on the front lines and some would battle on the high seas in the Navy, aboard the cruisers, battleships and aircraft carriers that were so critical to victory. Still others — including Herbert Small and his big brother Jim, would rain fire from above, taking the war to our enemies from the sky. All played their part in securing our freedom and American way of life.

In 1942, training to become pilots and fly missions in airplanes — from fighters to transports to bombers — involved five stages of training, the first four lasting roughly nine weeks each. There was a Pre-Flight stage that focused mainly on physical training and military discipline, similar to the common Basic Training in other branches of the service. This included three weeks of classroom study focusing on the mechanical aspects and physics of flight, which involved a good deal of mathematics, as well as teaching the men to start thinking like a pilot in three dimensions, rather than two, like an infantryman.

Then there was Primary Training, which taught them basic flying skills in small, relatively simple two-seater training planes. These planes were low horsepower aircraft meant to help pilot-trainees master the basics of flight before moving on to bigger and more powerful aircraft that would bring them closer to the "real thing" that they would eventually be flying into combat. These early stages were very intense and taken very seriously, and those who couldn't keep up with the rigorous pace of the training were "washed out" of the program.

From John R. McCrary's *First of the Many*, "A third of all the guys who try to be pilots are washed out in training. Another third drop out further along the line, because they don't like to fight. It's in the heart more than the guts. Those that do like to fight aren't necessarily killers, and those that don't like to fight aren't necessarily yellow. But if you don't like to fight, you don't belong in the Air Forces."

Training

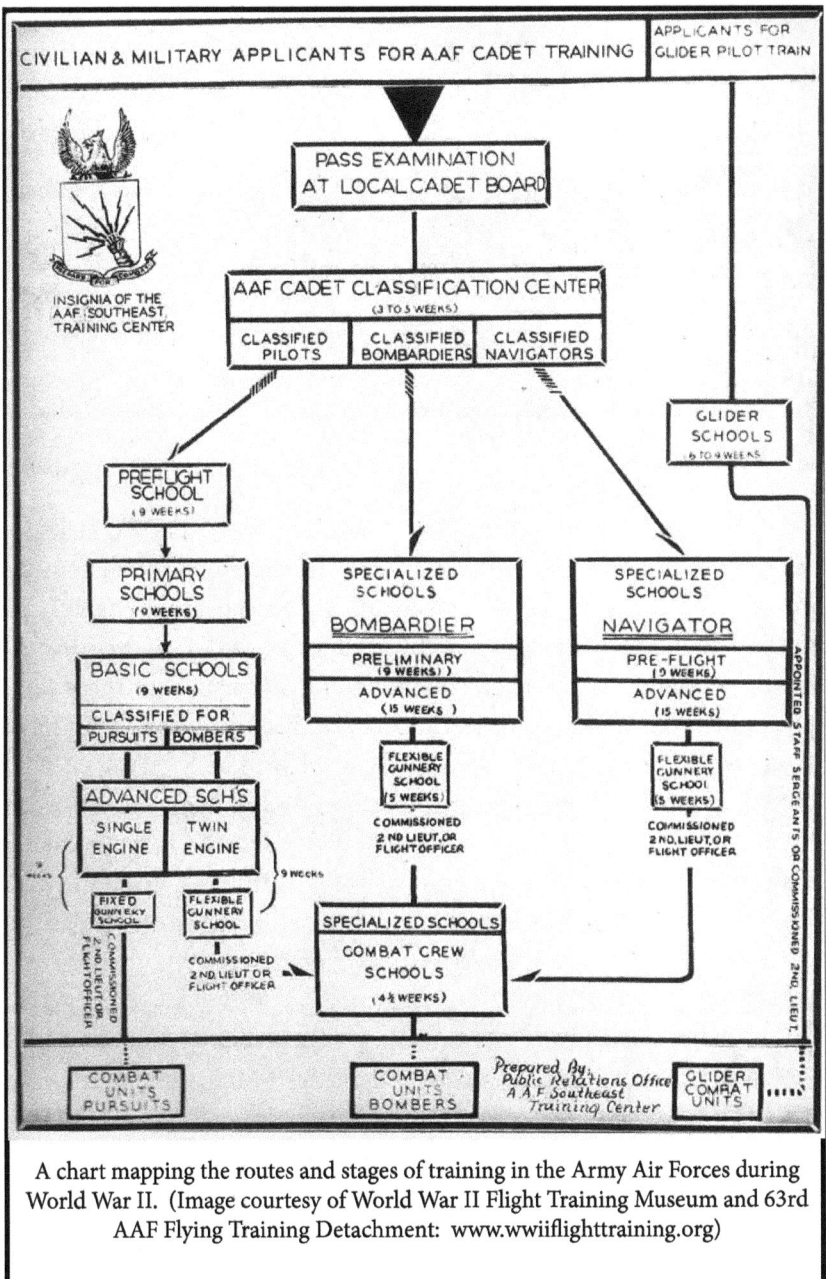

A chart mapping the routes and stages of training in the Army Air Forces during World War II. (Image courtesy of World War II Flight Training Museum and 63rd AAF Flying Training Detachment: www.wwiiflighttraining.org)

Bombs Away

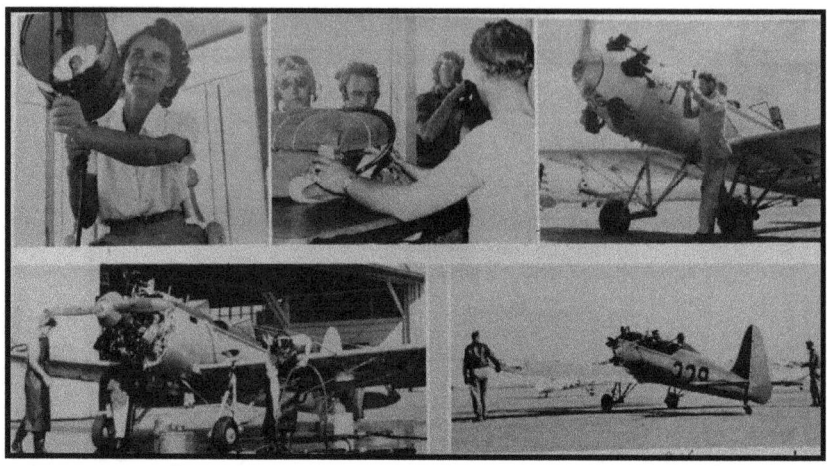

Various pictures from training at Sequoia Field in Visalia, CA from the cadet "yearbook" *Propwash*.   *(Courtesy of the Small Family)*

From Primary Training, the men moved on to Basic Flight Training for another nine weeks and moved on to larger and more powerful planes, such as the Vultee BT-13 Valiant. They also learned the difficult art of flying in formation, how to fly at night and to fly by their instruments, as well as aerial navigation and long-distance flying. These skills were critical for the men to learn, because they would be flying in all kinds of different conditions, and they needed to be a master of their aircraft in all situations. The airplanes they were flying were not the high-tech marvels of today — equipped with advanced radar, guidance systems and auto-pilot — that practically fly themselves. Even the B-17 Flying Fortress, which was the most advanced bomber of the day, required great strength, knowledge and skill of the crew in order to complete a mission.

From Basic Flight Training, they advanced for yet another nine weeks to Advanced Single-Engine or Advanced Multi-Engine training, depending on the type of aircraft they were training to serve in, which took their skills to the next level in even more powerful and complex aircraft. These aircraft would be more like the planes they would eventually fly into combat, though they were still a long way from the B-17s and B-24s they would eventually wind up in.   In these aircraft, they

Training

A Vultee BT-13 Valiant used for Basic Flight Training. (Stock Photo)

would begin to form the teams and crews that would go into battle together, training with navigators, bombardiers, radiomen and gunners to become efficient crews, ready to take the fight to their enemies.

After the Advanced stage came the final Transition stage, in which the various duties the pilots would be assigned emerged more definitively, with trainees separated into categories such as fighters, bombers, troop carriers or air transport, among others. The aircraftwere divided into different categories such as Light, Medium and Heavy, which meant pilots would wind up flying much different types of aircraft, from Dauntless Dive Bombers to Boeing B17 Flying Fortresses…and those in between, like the B-25 Mitchell medium bomber. This list also included the venerable B-24 Liberator, the other much-storied heavy bomber of the air war over Europe, brought to even further acclaim by the accomplished service of none other than Lt. Col. James "Jimmy" Stewart of Hollywood fame.

> **[Stewart's story is a fascinating one, if you care to check out the wonderful book *Jimmy Stewart, Bomber Pilot,* by Starr Smith. I was already a big fan of the Hollywood legend, and reading about his service took him to a different level for me.]**

Pilot trainees that washed out of any of the stages were often sent

Bombs Away

to other Army Air Force schools for training as bombardiers, gunners, navigators or radio operators, so as not to put those earlier months of training to waste. Others who washed out were sent back into the ranks of the regular Army for further training as infantrymen or for other duties, never to see the war from the air. From January 1941 through

Herb in uniform on leave for a break to get back to see his family in Sheffield. This is taken on the front lawn of the house on Salisbury Road, circa 1942. (Courtesy of the family.)

Training

August 1945, an impressive 191,654 cadets earned their pilot's wings; 132,993 cadet trainees washed out or were killed in unfortunate training accidents, resulting in a 40% total failure rate among those who began the training program. Pilot training was not for the faint of heart. Flying into combat wasn't either.

The final stages of training took place over the next fifteen to twenty-five weeks, based on in which phase of the war pilots had begun their training, and eventually included training in the real thing: B-17 Flying Fortresses or B-24 Liberators. In this stage they would get to know their plane — whichever plane they would be flying — with great intimacy. Crew members were cross-trained on multiple positions, such that even pilots could man the various guns, if necessary. If a crew member was killed or wounded, others needed to be able to step in to perform his duties in a pinch. They also were all familiar with the mechanics of the various systems within the plane, such as the oxygen system, heating system and fuel system, so other men besides the engineer could help with repairs in the heat of battle, if needed.

As for Herb's specific training journey, after his Pre-Flight Training in Merced, California, Herb was transferred to Sequoia Field in Visalia, California in the Fall of 1942 to attend the Eighth Army Air Forces Flying Training Detachment Visalia-Dinuba School of Aeronautics. This was his Primary Training location, where he would first take to the air in low-powered trainer planes and really begin his journey to become a pilot in a B-17 Flying Fortress for the United States Army Air Force. The B-17 was, at that point, one of the most modern and heavily armed bombers in the American arsenal -- and indeed the world -- and was a formidable weapon against our enemies in World War II.

In a letter sent home to younger sister Cece, postmarked just before Christmas 1942, one can sense how busy the pilot trainees were being kept, but also that Herb's family was never far from his thoughts. The letter is a Christmas card with the short message "Happy Christmas! Merry New Year!" printed inside, accompanied by an illustration of a mother dog enjoying her new puppies. Herb's message to his sister was eight simple words: "I knew this would 'tickle' you. Love Herb." It showed a bit of his dry sense of humor, with his appreciation for the humor found in the inversion of the typical "Merry Christmas and Happy New Year" wishes we are so familiar with and showed that he knew his little sister well enough to know she would also enjoy the little joke. It was a small thing, but I am sure that it meant a lot to both of them. It meant so much, in fact, that Cece saved that letter for the next eighty plus years, until her death in 2023, at almost ninety-five years old.

[An interesting thing that I learned late in the process of my research and writing was that the cadet-trainees at the Visalia training school produced what was essentially a yearbook -- called *Propwash* -- similar to that of a small high school or college, for the class that was going through training. It has descriptions of the various phases within the training, pictures of each of the instructors with biographies and captions for each. It also contains pictures of each of the cadets, with their own witty or philosophical caption underneath, as well as entries about the athletics, mess hall staff and entertainment on the base. Herb must have sent his home to his family, who saved it all of these years. Herb's caption simply read, "Don't know about that."]

The next stop for Herb's Basic Flight Training was Roswell, New Mexico, a location that would become infamous for and synonymous with aliens and conspiracy theories beginning just a few years later. But Herb wasn't there for aliens…he was there for the Roswell Army Flying School, where he would fly still larger and more powerful trainer planes, eventually earning promotion to 2nd Lieutenant and later his wings as a pilot in the Army Air Forces on May 20th, 1943.

Over the next four to five months, Herb received further train-

Training

Propwash, the "yearbook" style booklet produced for and by Herb's training class at Visalia-Dinuba School of Aeronautics. (Courtesy of the Small Family.)

ing during the Advanced Multi-Engine and Transition stages of training at bases in Ephrata, Washington, Rapid City, South Dakota and finally Brookdale, Florida. It was in these stages of training that the men really honed their craft and coalesced into the ten-man fighting crews they would become when deployed overseas. We know that he also passed through Scott Air Force Base in Western Illinois just east of St. Louis, because his radio operator Tech Sgt. William F. Laubenstein wrote in his memoirs, *A Quiet Hero: The true story of a WWII POW,* that they picked up their Fortress *Little Barney* at Scott Air Force Base before they eventually flew her to England.

In another letter back home, this time for "double credit" to his twin kid sisters Ann and Cece together, written during some rare down time during training, Herb displayed a wisdom beyond his twenty-two years, especially by today's standards. He wrote, on the subject of education and one of his sisters getting a perfect 100% score on a recent grammar exam:

> *Let me give you a tip, though. Don't work so much for marks in school as for an understanding of what you are doing. It's easy to get a hundred or close to it every day and then forget all about it next week. However, if you only get 85% on an exam and profit by your errors you'll remember it much longer.*

Herb goes on to discuss verb conjugations, Latin stems and English derivatives with his teenage sisters, which in itself is fairly remarkable. He also had some general updates about how things were going in his training:

> *There isn't much to talk about except that we're flying every day, going to ground school and athletics, as usual, and experiencing some unusual weather to a New Englander's way of thinking. Every night is cold but by ten o'clock it's warm again. At eleven thirty the wind starts to blow and keeps up till six or seven o'clock. The air is always full of sand and dust when there is wind...sometimes it blows so hard we can't fly.*

The full training process took just over a year, and by the Fall of 1943, 2nd Lt. Herbert W. Small was ready to enter the fight, and despite the United States not yet opening Stalin's much-desired Second Front on the ground by invading France, the war was nonetheless raging all over Europe and throughout most of the world, and the 8th Air Force was doing their part to help.

Training

[There is some popular criticism of the United States for supposedly waiting until June of 1944 to get into the war in Europe, which is simply a ludicrous argument that immediately shows the ignorance of anyone making such a claim. By 1944, American soldiers and Airmen had been fighting and dying in Africa, Sicily and Italy for many months. As early as November of 1942 with Operation Torch in Africa and July of 1943 with Operation Husky in Sicily, the United States was in the fight.]

For those men being sent to England, some crews went by boat, others ferried their own B-17s across the U.S., up through Newfoundland or Labrador, Canada and eventually made the final "hop" across the Atlantic, stopping in Iceland or Greenland, via the "Northern Route." Others took the "Southern Route," that ran through South America and Africa. Herbert Small's crew flew from Florida to Maine on the first leg of their trip. Radio operator William Laubenstein recalled; "Since these planes could not fly straight across the Atlantic Ocean, our first stop was in Bangor, Maine. The trip was exciting because we flew over Washington, DC and saw the U.S. Capitol Building. We were flying at a fairly low altitude, and it was a bright blue-sky day. The sights were breath-taking."

He went on to describe the rest of the trip; "We stayed in Bangor overnight and the next day we took off headed for Labrador, Canada. Our plane and crew then took off for Iceland. What a desolate piece of land; no trees, flat, rocky and cold. We were grounded there for some time. The people were kind to everyone and fed us well. After a week layover, the weather finally cleared enough for our trip across the "big pond" as I like to refer to the Atlantic Ocean, to Prestwick, Scotland. For me, the trip over all that water was scary, never having flown over water before. Of course, I was more than elated when we finally arrived safely. It is now in October of the year 1943. This date is very vivid in my mind because it was my birthday — October 14th."

Twin sisters Cece and Ann pose with their mother Cecelia in nearly the same spot as Herb's uniform photo.   (Photo courtesy of the family.)

[In another happy coincidence for the family, both twin sisters, Cece and Ann, would go on to marry fine gentlemen named Joe; Joseph Kay and Joseph Finn, respectively. Maybe it's true that twins think alike.]

Training

*****

The atmosphere on the boats and in the bombers for the men heading to war would have been very different from that on the trains and busses at the start of training twelve to fifteen months earlier. It was now one of anticipation and anxiety…fear and excitement. The many months of hard work and training were all about to come to fruition, their skills put to the test as they leaped into action.

The letters sent back home would likely have been very different then, too, as the men knew they were going to be putting themselves very much in harm's way, and they perhaps contemplated the likelidhood that many of them would not be coming back. A much more serious tone would have come from men who were now much more serious themselves. Gone, at least partially, were the boys who signed up for war, replaced by men trained as pilots, navigators, radiomen, flight engineers, gunners and a dozen other support jobs on the ground at air bases.

Herb was assigned to the 384th Bombardment Group (Heavy) on November 5th, 1943, and specifically to the 544th Bombardment Squadron (Heavy) within the 384th, which was stationed in England at Grafton-Underwood Airbase AAF Station 106. William Laubenstein commented in his memoirs: "On October 15, 1943, we boarded a train for Grafton-Underwood. This is the base from which we made our missions. When we arrived in England, our pilot, Mr. [2nd Lt. Earl] Allison, informed us that we were already assigned to the 384th [Group] 544th [Squadron] bomb group. We were near Kettering, England which is a city about five miles from our base. This city was not too happy when our planes took off for a mission at 5:30 or 6:00 AM."

It wasn't long before Herb was at Grafton-Underwood headed down the runway for his first mission on November 16th, only eleven days after he was assigned, seated in the co-pilot's chair next to seasoned pilot Captain Randolph G. E. "Moose" Jacobs, headed to drop his first bombs on a Molybdenum mine in Norway.

Jacobs' crew, with whom Herb only flew his first two missions, was not the crew he had trained with, flew across the North Atlantic with or that he was part of when he was assigned to the 384th. It was common practice to have newly arrived pilots fly their first couple of missions as the co-pilot with men who had some combat mission experience in order to get a better idea what the "real thing" would be like. It wasn't until Herb's third mission on December 13, 1943 that he joined the crew that he'd mostly fly with for his next twenty-four missions. Sometimes there were subs for one crew member or another because of health or other reasons, but generally the nine men he flew with on December 13th would go on to be his regular crew for the remainder of his service.

Until his final mission.

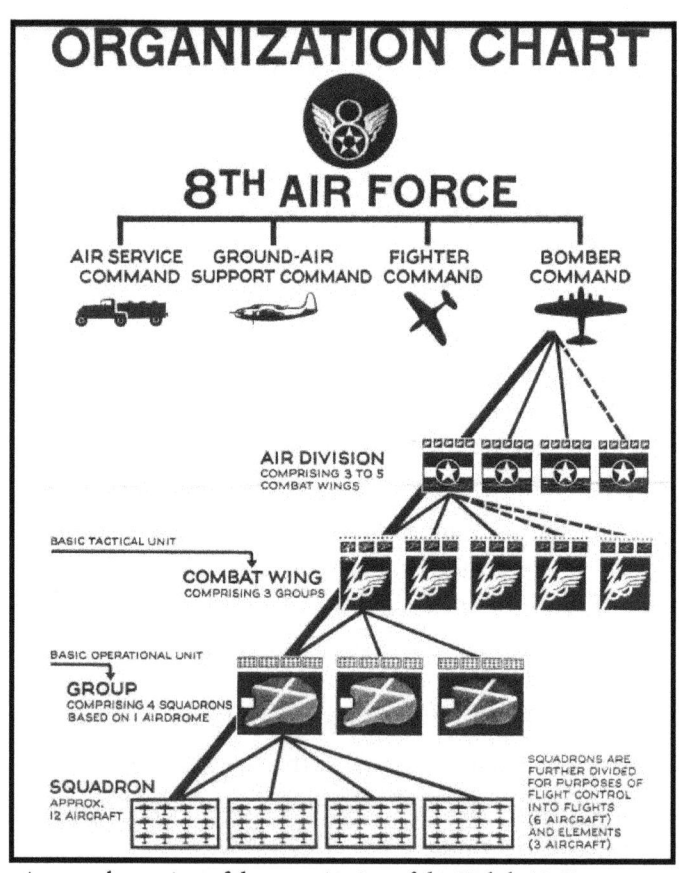

ORGANIZATION CHART

8TH AIR FORCE

- AIR SERVICE COMMAND
- GROUND-AIR SUPPORT COMMAND
- FIGHTER COMMAND
- BOMBER COMMAND

AIR DIVISION COMPRISING 3 TO 5 COMBAT WINGS

BASIC TACTICAL UNIT
COMBAT WING COMPRISING 3 GROUPS

BASIC OPERATIONAL UNIT
GROUP COMPRISING 4 SQUADRONS BASED ON 1 AIRDROME

SQUADRON APPROX. 12 AIRCRAFT

SQUADRONS ARE FURTHER DIVIDED FOR PURPOSES OF FLIGHT CONTROL INTO FLIGHTS (6 AIRCRAFT) AND ELEMENTS (3 AIRCRAFT)

A general overview of the organization of the Eighth Air Force.

Grafton-Underwood Airbase

3

Herb was officially assigned to the 544th Bomber Squadron of the 384th Bombardment Group (Heavy) on November 5th, 1943, and would soon be up in the air on his first mission, just eleven days later on November 16th. However, he arrived at Grafton-Underwood in late October of 1943, a week or two earlier, so he had a little bit of time to settle into the base and receive some additional training before his first mission. He arrived at the base as a 2nd Lieutenant, which meant he would be quartered with the officers, with somewhat nicer accommodations than the enlisted men. Even so, they were certainly a far cry from the Ritz-Carlton!

In the years 1942 through 1945, the eastern-central area of England, known as East Anglia — an area no bigger than the state of Vermont, comprised of Norfolk, Cambridgeshire, Bedford, Hertfordshire and Essex counties — transformed from a charming, sleepy countryside into a bustling hotbed of wartime aviation activity. Seemingly overnight, United States Army Air Force bases sprung up all over the region, with 130 British and American bases in total at the peak in June of 1944. Bases were designated for four main purposes; Bombardment Groups, comprised mostly of B-17 Flying Fortresses and B-24 Liberators; Fighter

Bombs Away

Groups, featuring P-38 Lightnings, P-47 Thunderbolts, and beginning in 1944, P-51 Mustangs; and lastly, Headquarters and Reconnaissance outfits.

The weather in East Anglia was invariably cold and damp throughout all but the summer months, and the small coal burning stoves that were in most of the Nissen Hut living quarters did a poor job of heating them, especially given the very limited coal ration assigned to each hut per week. Scavenging coal from the base stockpile or by other means became a serious pursuit for some of the men, in the never-ending quest to fend off the cold.

The region was peppered with bases, in formerly serene villages like Alconbury, Bassingbourn and Chelveston; Deenethorpe, Eye and Framingham; Grafton-Underwood and Halesworth…all the way to Snetterton Heath, Thorpe Abbots and Wormingford. Not to mention Thurleigh, Molesworth and Polebrook, along with dozens of others. The

The modern village of Grafton-Underwood, UK. (Stock Photo.)

Grafton-Underwood Airbase

little villages nearby each of these bases became the home-away-from-home for tens of thousands of Army Air Force personnel, from senior officers and pilots to mechanics and mess hall cooks, and everyone in between. They even had an Oscar-winning Hollywood movie-star-turned-bomber-pilot...but more on that later.

[Thorpe Abbotts has come to some notoriety recently because of the popularity of the Apple TV+ series *"Masters of the Air,"* which does an incredible job of depicting the experiences of a heavy bomber group based in England during World War II.]

In 2007, Smithsonian Magazine writer John Fleischman described the East Anglia region as, "Flat, heavily agricultural, and perfectly placed for launching mass formations of propellor-driven, high-altitude heavy bombers deep into German territory, East Anglia was the cannon's mouth for the U.S. Army's Eighth Air Force." It was a perfect staging area for air attacks on Germany and other enemy held territory,

Grafton-Underwood,UK. Circa 1943. (Courtesy of Paul Teal and Sam Coleman.)

Flak Dancer

Bombs Away

with a relatively short distance to travel to find targets and far away from heavily populated areas like London or other major cities.

Today, Grafton-Underwood is still a small, quaint village about sixty-five miles north of London with a population of roughly 140 people, much like it was before the war and the influx of "Yanks." Just north of the village there remains today a mere shadow of the airbase that between 1943 and 1945 was a sprawling five-hundred-acre complex housing approximately 3,000 Army Air Force personnel of the Eighth Air Force. The complex featured a cinema, hospital, officers' clubs and chapel, as well as athletic fields and a skeet-shooting range, along with the numerous barracks and other buildings necessary to sustain a bustling military base during a time of war. For after-hours entertainment for those who weren't officers, the base also had the "Aero Club," the "Zebra Club" and the "Privates' and Corporals' Bar."

The airfield was originally constructed in 1941 as a satellite field for use by the RAF (Britain's Royal Air Force) in the event that other airfields were knocked out by enemy action, and it was literally carved out of the English countryside for this purpose. It was done with the intention of also leaving as much of the extremely valuable farmland active for food production. In a small country like Great Britain, there wasn't enough farmland to spare that they could just give big swaths of it to the military for their bases. Every farmable acre was critical to keeping the populace and the fighting men fed.

The English bases used an entirely different design to their construction compared to the typical layout of American military bases, which are often built on a large, wide-open tract of land with no other purpose than to be a military base. In *One Last Look: A Sentimental Journey to the Eighth Air Force Heavy Bomber Bases of World War II in England*, Philip Kaplan and Rex A. Smith wrote: "…the most striking feature of these English air stations was the seeming irrationality of their design. They did not sit upon the land neatly, as American bases did. They sprawled upon it, were entangled in its features, and some of their parts were entirely disconnected from the rest." Kaplan and Smith went

Grafton-Underwood Airbase

on: "They were unusual bases built to fill the needs of unusual times. Now those bases and times are both long gone, and their kind will not be seen again."

The rationale for the seemingly unusual layout and design of the bases goes back to two main factors: the need for the farmland to be preserved and for the barracks to be distributed throughout the base rather than being clumped together, for reasons of safety we'll explore later.

The barracks buildings themselves were mainly canvas and wood structures, but some of them were of more permanent brick construction, such as the mess halls, officers' clubs and hospital. Later, the well-known Nissen Huts were added, which were similar to the more well-known Quonset Huts (used primarily in the Pacific theater) in their simple but effective construction.

The Grafton-to-Brigstock Road bisected the base, running south to north out of the village of Grafton-Underwood, with mainly the runways and hangars to the west of the road and the rest of the base to the east. It was a short ride down that same road to the village of Grafton-Underwood, and the men frequently rode their bicycles into town to go to the pubs or other shops, or even just to visit with locals, whom in many cases they had befriended.

The Grafton-Underwood base was the first airfield in England to receive a unit from the Eighth Air Force, and the first outfit to inhabit the base was the 15th Bomber Squadron, who moved in on May 12th, 1942, but remained there less than a month before moving to nearby Molesworth on June 9th. The 97th Bomber Group arrived next on July 6th to begin operations with the Boeing B-17 Flying Fortress. Over the next several months, Station 106, as the base was designated, was occupied by the 305th Bomb Group in September of 1942 and then the 96th Bomb Group, until finally on May 25th, 1943, the 384th Bombardment Group (Heavy) became the final unit assigned there through the end of the war in 1945.

According to a September 26, 1977 article by the Evening Telegraph, "some 326 missions were flown from the base by the 'Mighty 8th' including the first and last bombing flights of the war." The article was

Bombs Away

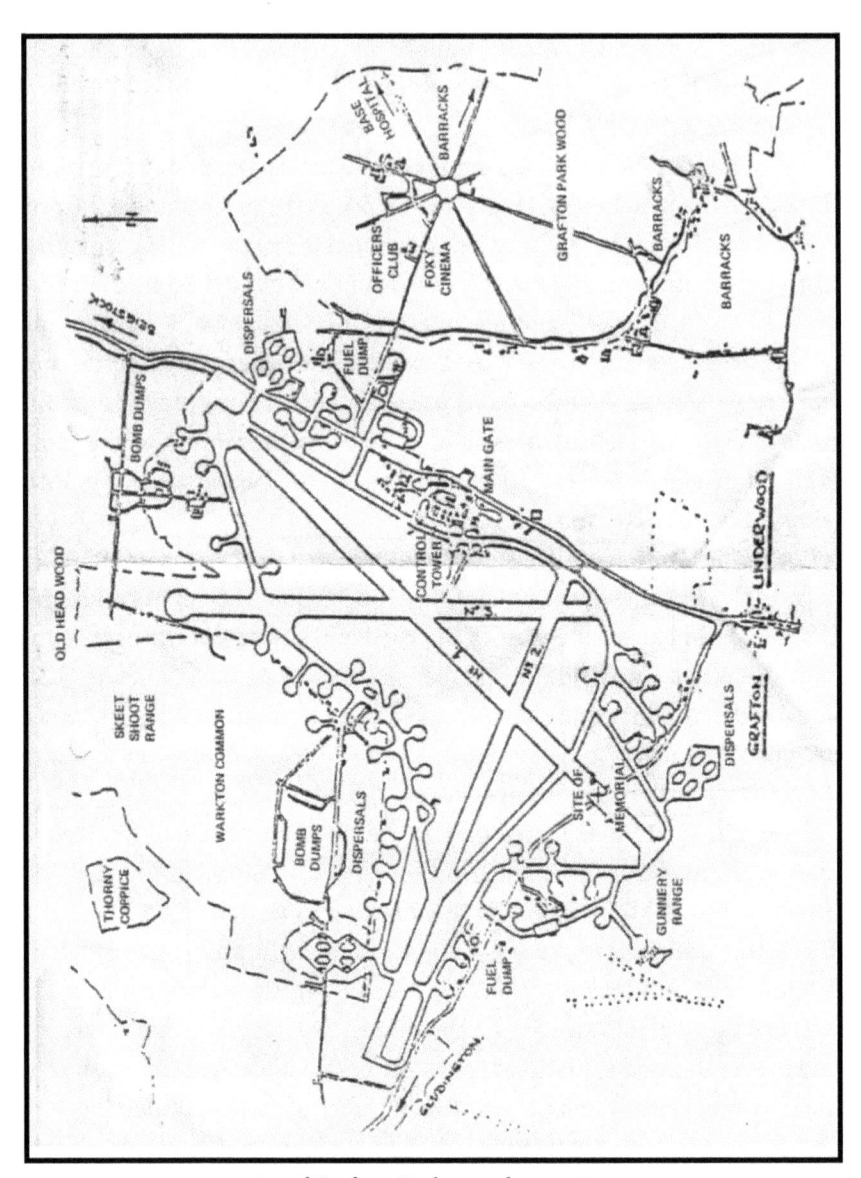

Map of Grafton-Underwood, circa 1944.
(Courtesy of Mikayla Leech.)

Grafton-Underwood Airbase

B-17G Sea Hag goes off the runway into the quagmire of mud.
(Courtesy of 384thBombGroup.com)

written to commemorate the dedication of a memorial to the Eighth Air Force in the village of Grafton-Underwood. The memorial was unveiled by William Dolan, an 81-year-old veteran fighter pilot during World War I who also volunteered for World War II and served as the Group Combat Intelligence Officer at Grafton-Underwood, despite the fact that he was past the age at which he could be called up for military service. Mr. Dolan was quoted in the article, giving readers a sense of how the Americans and the local Brits felt about each other: "We were here for almost three years and this [memorial] is a reminder of all the friendship, kindness and understanding given to us by the local people. The village is still beautiful but the people make it what it is." It's hard to mistake or miss the affection he still had for the residents of the village of Grafton-Underwood, even all those years later.

The airbase was broken up into fourteen individual sites, with Site No. 1 being the airfield itself, fittingly, since that was the main reason

Bombs Away

they were all there. Occupying the entire west side of the base, Site No. 1 included the areas where crews would work on the airplanes, hangars and repair sheds, the Control Tower (Watch Office), various equipment stores, flight and squadron offices and dozens of other buildings serving numerous critical functions. There was even a skeet-shooting range for the men to blow off steam and practice marksmanship at the same time.

Sites 4, 5, 6, 8, 9, 10 and 11, which were spread out widely across the base, were dedicated to Officers' Quarters, Sergeants' Quarters and Airmen's Barracks, with latrines and a picket post (guard shed) at each. The bases were intentionally built with a widespread plan of design, so that living quarters were not too near the runways, and the living and communal quarters were divided up and spread out. This was done on purpose so that potential airstrikes by the enemy would be less likely to inflict heavy damage to the crews and support personnel, because they weren't heavily concentrated in one particular area. To this same end, the barracks were often woven neatly into the landscape and amongst small groups of trees around the base, which made them more difficult to discern when viewed from German aerial reconnaissance planes or bombers.

In One Last Look, by Philip Kaplan, the author recounts the words of Ray Wild in his description of the base at Podington: "The runways were built right into the farm, and the farmer was still farming it. He'd be there farming when we left on a raid, and he'd still be farming when we came back." This was common among the landowners who essentially loaned or leased their land to the military for use as bases. Unfortunately, the landowners and their farming activities weren't always in perfect harmony with the military function of the bases. One consequence of the farming that caused a lot of unrest at Grafton-Underwood was mud. And lots of it.

At Grafton-Underwood in late 1943, the mud around the base was quickly going from a general nuisance to a very serious problem. Vehicles were tracking the mud onto the runways and hardstands, which was then getting stuck on the wheels of the B-17s. Base Commander Col. Dale O. Smith wrote in *Screaming Eagle: Memoirs of a B-17 Group*

Grafton-Underwood Airbase

The Foxy Theatre before (T) and during (B) a show. On top, showing *By Hook or By Crook,* featuring Red Skelton.
(Courtesy of 384thBombGroup.com)

Bombs Away

Commander: "There were instances of landing gear sticking in the up position when the mud froze. Something had to be done and soon." And as the man in charge, it was up to him.

A big part of the problem was the muddy roads and the large trucks that were constantly using them, squishing and tracking the mud everywhere. As the new 384th Commanding Officer starting in late November of 1943, Col. Smith made an interesting discovery regarding the muddy state of the roads that he shared in his memoirs; "One day I dug down in the mud on our roads and discovered that under the mud was a lane of concrete pavement, with occasional concrete turnouts for passing." He implemented a base-wide program of shoveling off the several inches of mud from the many miles of roads on the base, as well as a strict policy of exclusively using the concrete turnouts instead of passing on the unpaved areas, which he believed had solved the problem.

However, a big contributor to the mud problem was that Grafton-Underwood Air Base had its own eccentric landlord in the form of British aristocrat the Duke of Buccleuch. The Duke leased to them the land the base was built upon, but still actively employed much of his surrounding land in farming. He had his farm workers moving soil — mostly mud, due to the inclement weather — from one of his fields to

Some of the many bicycles on base at Grafton-Underwood. (Courtesy of 384thBombGroup.com).

Grafton-Underwood Airbase

another, frequently traversing the base in the process. As the large farm trucks travelled along the newly uncovered concrete roads, they oozed mud out the back and re-covered the roads with mud in a matter of days. A power struggle ensued between Col. Smith and the Duke, who was officially a member of the Royal Family. Smith eventually prevailed in the end, somewhat to his own surprise, but the whole ordeal added unnecessary stress to an already difficult time.

According to *As Briefed: a family history of the 384th Bombardment Group*, by Capt. Walter E. Owens, "By November [1943], anyone on the station was ready to give Grafton back to the Indians — or, rather, back to the Duke of Buccleuch. And by November the name of the station had been changed unofficially from "Grafton-Underwood" to "Grafton-Undermud." Col. Smith solved the problem of the near-relentless mud and also worked hard to improve other living conditions for the men, including dramatically improving the food that was being served on the base. This understandably led to an overall improvement in morale throughout the 384th.

Philip Kaplan and Rex Alan Smith had more to say about the mud in *One Last Look*: "Another problem is mud. When it rains, all unpaved roads, paths, and barracks areas become gooey quagmires, and it rains a lot. Also, the latrines and showers are in Nissen huts separate from the barracks; the mess halls and other such base facilities are, in most cases, at a considerable distance from the housing sites, and especially in cold or muddy weather this inconvenience is the inspiration for a good deal of inventive and colorful language."

Site 7, located in the southwest corner of the airbase, was reserved for the WAAF (Women's Auxiliary Air Force) Airwomen's Barracks, presumably a safe distance away from the young men who were separated from their sweethearts back home and needed no additional temptation. The Sick Quarters — Site 12 — were located to the northeast, and the two sewage treatment areas, Sites 13 and 14, were located to the far east and south of the base respectively…hopefully downwind.

The remaining sites, Site 2 and Site 3, were the "Communal" sites

Bombs Away

— essentially the equivalent of the center of town back home — and featured a large array of buildings of a common-use nature, such as the chapel, mess halls, showers, a grocery store, dining rooms and a cinema named "The Foxy," which featured popular movies from the biggest stars of the day and was well-attended by the men. (Located at Site 3 - Part of Building 229). Also in these areas were the athletic fields and basketball courts where the men engaged in all manner of athletics, whenever the not-always-cooperative English weather allowed. The communal sites were placed to be conveniently accessible to most of the living quarters sites, so that getting to and from meals, showers, meetings and social functions wasn't too arduous a chore for the men. The men would often walk or bike to the chapel, showers, grocery store or mess hall when needed.

Because of the widely dispersed set-up of the base, bicycles were a very common mode of transportation for the men. For some it might have been a ten- or twenty-minute walk just to get to the showers, the mess hall or the Officers' or Enlisted Men's clubs. Bikes were a great way to travel, and they were in such high demand that they sold out in many areas of England when the Americans showed up, no doubt to the chagrin of the locals who had been using them all along. To the reserved British, the bicycles were no toys, rather a standard and steadfast means of transportation.

The enlisted men, or non-commissioned officers, lived in separate quarters from the officers, typically with more men per building than the officers. The buildings were often Nissen Huts, made of corrugated metal and shaped into a half-circle, like a giant drainage culvert cut in half. They came in various sizes and were named after the Canadian engineer who designed them, Lt. Col. Peter N. Nissen. They were cold and didn't offer the best protection against the elements, but they were cheap and easy to construct and move around, so the men made do as best they could. The huts usually featured a large potbellied stove in the middle to heat the barracks in inclement weather, and the larger huts could accommodate ten or more bunks.

Grafton-Underwood Airbase

Exterior of a typical Nissen Hut. (Courtesy of 384thBombGroup.com)

[I wonder if it ever occurred to Herb Small or struck him funny that he had come 3,300 miles across the Atlantic Ocean from Sheffield only to be once again living in cold, overcrowded living quarters with a pot-bellied stove as his main source of heat.]

Owens's *As Briefed* offers a tongue-in-cheek opinion on the subject of the English weather: "Winter in the English Midlands must have been what the bears had in mind when they developed the custom of devoting a part of their time to hibernation. Dawn in the middle of the morning, darkness by mid-afternoon, a continuous dripping fog...". Coming from New England, Herb Small would not have been a stranger to unpleasant and challenging weather, but I can only imagine how those from some of the warmer U.S. climates adjusted to their new environs.

The living quarters, often the Nissen huts, were dark, usually coated with mud from boots and smelled of dirty, damp clothing, cigarettes and unwashed men too tired to make the trek to the showers after a long day. The men slept on Army cots, both English and American, which were described as stiff and as having the supports in all the wrong

Officers Club Mess at Grafton-Underwood, with Red Cross volunteers.
(Courtesy of 384thBombGroup.com)

places for comfortable sleeping. Men often struggled with blankets, pillows and other improvised items in trying to find comfortable sleeping positions.

The combination of officers (lieutenants, captains, majors and higher ranks) and enlisted men (privates, corporals and sergeants) could have been problematic amongst the crews, but most sources I have come across have stated that the distinctions of rank seldom were of any real importance to the men, especially once they were up on a mission. Of the ten-man B-17 crews, typically four men were officers — the pilot, co-pilot, navigator and bombardier — the rest, including the radio man, engineer and all of the gunners, were typically enlisted men. It wasn't a one-hundred percent hard and fast rule, evidenced by the fact that Lt. Herb Small flew at least two missions (384th BG missions #76 & #86) as a tail gunner. (It turns out this was due to a specific policy introduced by

Grafton-Underwood Airbase

the Base Commander Col. Dale O. Smith in 1944...more on that later.)

[For those interested in learning more about the 384th Bombardment Group, please visit the incredible website www.384thBombGroup.com to see an unbelievable collection of information about 384th personnel, missions, aircraft, mission records, photos, statistics and other records. It is by far the most useful and valuable source of data I have found for this book, and the best website dedicated to a military unit I have ever seen. Please consider becoming a member or supporting their great work in any way you are able.]

In his book *Jimmy Stewart: Bomber Pilot,* Starr Smith wrote: "Rank among the combat crews, especially overseas, was observed, but practiced with a casual we're-all-in-this-thing-together attitude." He went on to say that "Friendships among crew members formed quickly and often endured throughout the war and into many years of civilian life. Crew members met as young men. They trained together, lived together, fought together, cried together, drank together — died together."

When they were not training and not on missions, the ranks rarely mixed socially, with separate living quarters, mess halls, showers, latrines and social clubs for drinking and/or dancing. However, when they were in the air, they were a team and functioned as one unit, with one purpose: the successful completion of the mission at hand. And on that team, the pilot was the undisputed leader and commander. It was his ship, and what he said was what the men did. With that exception, rank meant very little in the heat of battle. The authority of the pilot was so respected and the men's discipline so strong that one story tells of a B-17 on fire after being struck from anti-aircraft flak; the ball turret gunner was so disciplined that he requested permission from the pilot to exit his turret as the fire raged around him, threatening to cook him alive!

De Rumble Izer

Bombs Away

*****

Life at Grafton-Underwood consisted mainly of training for missions, prepping for missions and going on actual missions, but there was also some down-time for the men, since they did not have missions every day. Down-time gave them a chance to engage in recreation on the base, such as football, basketball, baseball and other sports, as well as to explore the local villages, of which there were plenty. The men frequented the Foxy Theatre and Officers' or Enlisted Men's clubs, and there were Red Cross volunteers that organized dances and other social events… sometimes the Red Cross volunteers simply passed out treats like donuts and coffee to over-worked and exhausted airmen and ground crews.

The nearby villages provided some much-needed distraction, as they contained two timeless draws for young men with spare time on their hands and spare money in their pockets: pubs and women. The pubs served mainly warm beer, which no doubt took some getting used to for the Americans, but warm beer is still beer, and it has the same effect. It probably also helped to break the ice with the young British women, who in many cases were friendly with and dated the airmen, and in some cases — roughly 50,000 cases, in fact — married them. The local villagers also needed some time to get used to the Yanks, who were suddenly everywhere, with their multitude of funny-sounding accents, snazzy uniforms and boisterous attitudes, no doubt a shock to the system for the well-mannered and more reserved Brits.

Author Kevin Wilson spoke of it very well in his excellent work, *Blood and Fears*: "The American airman was truly a glamorous figure in drab wartime Britain. From his neat little 'overseas' cap to his shiny brown shoes he spoke of a different world, a land of plenty where confidence came with the territory. The closest most [English] girls had been to American manhood in their conservative pre-war existence was the silver screen, where the macho charm of actors such as Jimmy Stewart and Clark Gable had stolen their hearts."

[Little did most of the local girls know that if they

Grafton-Underwood Airbase

just kept their eyes open and had a bit of luck on their side, they might just get to see one or both of the famous Hollywood stars, as they were both serving in the Eighth Air Force in England at the time!]

From 1941 to 1945, some three million American military service personnel passed through Great Britain, with the U.S. Army Air Forces making up roughly 500,000 of that number. That massive influx of mostly young, healthy, confident and well-paid men was a boon for the young ladies in England, and a frustration for the young men, I would think. Most of the young women had never imagined being surrounded by so many interesting, handsome and dashing young men. They met at the movies, dances and concerts, and the Yanks spoiled the girls with attention and gifts. It was the age-old sport of men courting (or chasing) women…and the game was afoot!

In the official 384th Bomber Group history, *As Briefed*, Capt. Walter E. Owens described both life on the base at Grafton-Underwood and the interactions the men had with the local people of the area. When the men first arrived, he writes, "There was a week's restriction for the ground men, and during that time they were to learn more of Army security, more of formation flying, more of those things that had been drummed into their minds back in the states. There also were a few new items, such as what not to do in an English pub. 'Remember, the English like their beer at room temperature,' everyone was told. 'So don't make a wry face and shove it back across the counter with the suggestion that they put it back in the horse.'" The 384th unit history goes on to add "In the pubs they tried mild and bitters and had 'a go' at darts and skittles, learned — to the discouragement of native patrons who already were faced with a strictly rationed beer supply — to drink fast in the hour or two before the barmaid draped the pump handles and announced: "Towel's up."

However, there was another, more endearing side to these men stationed thousands of miles from home in a new and strange land besides the beer drinking womanizers you may be picturing. Many of

Sgt. Delbert P. McNasty on duty at Grafton-Underwood.
(Photo courtesy of James Traylor and Mikayla Leech.)

them truly befriended the locals and were in return welcomed into their homes to share meals, friendship and affection. These were, after all, still very young men — boys really — who were often homesick for the family and the life they had left behind; mothers, fathers, siblings and sweethearts were only the stuff of letters. Remember, many of the men had never been far away from home before, and certainly not this far; safe to say some might be homesick. The locals became their surrogate moms, dads and siblings for a time, and no doubt the Brits drew a similar benefit from the American guests, as well, since many of their own husbands, fathers, sons and brothers were off fighting the war themselves.

I have learned that where men are to be found, Man's Best Friend can usually also be found, and Grafton-Underwood was no exception to this rule. The men befriended and cared for many canine companions who wandered onto the base and into their lives and hearts. *As Briefed* describes in detail one such pooch, affectionately named "Sgt. Delbert P. McNasty." "[He] wasn't the only dog on the base, but he came of the

Grafton-Underwood Airbase

most doubtful extraction and he had the most unpredictable personality and he created enough disturbance for all the rest of them put together. As a dog, he wasn't much — just a hunk of black hair with gimlet eyes and ragged, drooping ears. But as a cog in the communal life at Grafton-Underwood he was on a level with all the brass that sat around the staff tables determining policy and establishing precedent."

> **[In the many pictures of the 384th featured on the excellent website www.384thBomb Group.com, one can occasionally see dogs posing with the men as they were photographed, just like they were part of the crew. Personally, this endears me even further to these men of whom I've already become a big fan.]**

Delbert McNasty had joined the 384th by wandering into the orderly room of the 544th Squadron while they were training back at Wendover Air Base in Utah. He wound up staying for the remainder of the phase training and making the hop "across the pond" to England with the air echelon.

As men form particularly strong bonds with their fellow broth-

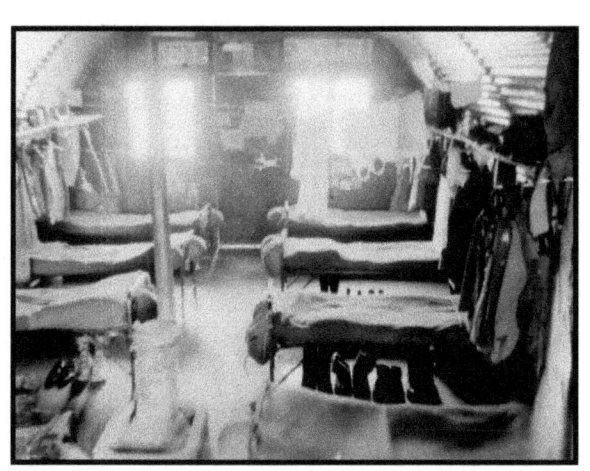

Interior of a Nissen Hut with a coke stove in the middle.
(Courtesy of Paul Teal and Sam Coleman.)

Pleasure Bent

ers in arms, so too do they form strong bonds with their beloved dogs, and I strongly believe that the dogs develop a strong attachment for the humans who love and care for them. The 384th unit history *As Briefed* makes specific mention that the frequent loss of men from the 384th may have had an unknowable effect on the poor pup, who was certainly not able to understand why people were disappearing from his life with such regularity. How could one possibly console such a creature, as the consolers themselves may very well be the next ones to disappear from poor Delbert's life without explanation? It's no surprise that a dog experiencing frequent loss and trauma like that might develop some odd personality quirks. Can dogs experience a version of PTSD? I would wager they can.

The final entry in the unit history about Delbert McNasty seems to tell of a fitting end to his part in the story of the 544th Squadron: "Over in the 544th site Private Delbert McNasty stayed around Barracks S-1 for a while, but [1st Lt. Jesse Dee] Hausenfluck [Jr.] (the man who had befriended, cared for and smuggled the dog to England) and his crew didn't come back. The next day he stayed in with the boys of Lieutenant [Thomas J.] Estes' crew, but he kept running back once in a while to see if Kennedy or Everton or McKenzie or any of the others had showed up. Finally, after about a week, he took off with a Red Cross Girl and no one ever saw him around the base after that." Ironically, it was likely the dream of many an airman to enjoy suffering such a fate.

An even bigger draw for the men than the local villages was London. It was a bigger city than most of the men had ever set eyes upon, and it was only a two-hour train ride away. The promise of big city liquor, gambling, women and nightlife was a huge treat for them, and some took advantage as often as they could. There was even the curious and sometimes tempting draw of the infamous "Piccadilly Commandos," as many of the more aggressive London prostitutes around Piccadilly Square became known. As long as the men were back on base before their passes were up, they were usually okay with the higher-ups. In a time and occupation where death was literally all around them, many of them — rightfully so — lived every moment to its fullest and made the most of every bit of free time they had. For the air crews, no one knew when their number might be called and their ticket punched, never to come home again.

From all that I have learned about Herbert Small, I don't believe he would have been all that interested in the nightlife of London or the pursuit of cheap liquor and easy women. Those things weren't for him. Several sources have described Herb as a very serious and thoughtful young man, who was driven to do his duty and fight for his country. Herb was there to fly, and he already had a sweetheart back home named Alice Kline, whom he knew from Great Barrington, Massachusetts, the nearest town just north of Sheffield. Their plan from some sources, reportedly, was to get married when Herb returned home from the war, and he had even given her a pair of his "wings" after becoming a pilot, possibly as a promissory token. Other family sources counter the claim of possible wedding plans, saying that the couple's plan was more like "a plan to make plans" when Herb returned from the war, and that they were trying not to look too far ahead, for obvious reasons. Alice was about a year and a half younger than Herb, and unfortunately the details of how they met and became involved have been lost to history. It is possible that Alice moved to London for a time as a Women's Auxiliary Volunteer to be nearer to Herb, though that has also been disputed by her surviving family. I was also unable to find any record of her being an official volunteer with any of the Women's Auxiliary groups.

There is a great story told in *Jimmy Stewart: Bomber Pilot*, by Starr Smith, that seems to be an apt summary of life on an Eighth Air Force base, including the relationship between officers and enlisted men, and speaks to the incredible character of Jimmy Stewart himself. The story is of an incident of theft on his base at Tibenham, out of which he flew numerous missions as a pilot on B-24 Liberators. Apparently, a keg of beer from the Officers' Club had gone missing, which had the "higher ups" in quite a state of agitation. It was at a time of particularly low morale for the men, so it was not surprising to then Major James M.

Bombs Away

Stewart that something like this small act of defiance could occur. He walked into the living quarters of one of his flight crews with whom he was very familiar, in an attempt to get his perpetually cold feet warmed up, a struggle for which he was well-known amongst his men.

He entered the hut and approached the stove to warm himself, noticing that the men were having a drink. He wandered over to a pile of blankets on a cot nearby and picked up the corner of one of the blankets, discovering the missing keg. Without saying a word, he nonchalantly strode to a nearby shelf and removed the metal cup from a canteen that was stored there. He poured himself a beer from the keg and sat down amongst the men, slowly drinking the beer and warming himself by the stove. When his cup was empty, he repeated the process for a second cup, commenting on how good the English beer was, all the while, the men nervously waited for an angry rebuke.

The author, Starr Smith relates; "After a while, he said quietly, *'Fellows, someone stole a keg of beer from the officers club a few days ago.'* He looked around. *'Ah—you guys hear anything about that?'* We shook our heads. We said we hadn't heard anything about it. Stewart shook the last drop of dark beer out of my empty cup that he had been drinking from. *'I thought not,'* he said. He wiped the lip of it with his hand. Then he put the cup back on my canteen and carefully placed it where he got it, on the shelf over my bunk.

"He walked over to the beer keg and pulled the blanket back over it. He tucked the blanket around the keg carefully. You couldn't see the keg in the pile of blankets anymore…

"Stewart cleared his throat and said, *'I know that Lieutenant Wright's crew doesn't know anything about this. I'm certain they didn't have a thing to do with stealing a keg of beer.'*

"He turned, wiping his mouth with the back of his hand. He zipped up his jacket and walked out of the front door without saying another word."

Major Stewart never reprimanded or punished the men…indeed he likely never spoke of it to anyone until after the war, knowing that the men were just letting off a little bit of steam and trying to cope as best

Grafton-Underwood Airbase

"Keeping warm around the stove in a Nissen Hut." Randy Jacobs and two of his crew having a laugh over coffee and a smoke. I believe the man on the right is 1st Lt. Eugene A. Boger and the man on the left is possibly 1st. Lt. John Q. Curtin, though I am not certain. (Courtesy of 348thBombGroup.com).

they could with the difficulties and deprivations of war and life on the base.

Life at Grafton-Underwood, and probably most of the bases in England, was not easy for the men. Those stationed at these air bases did what soldiers, sailors and airmen always seem to do; they made the best of things; they rolled with the punches; they sucked it up and did what they had to do to get by. The clever and creative men often made improvised improvements to their quarters, such as commandeering bigger stoves and more coal, building shelves, buying radios and putting up "pin-up" art on the walls of their huts. Anything to make life away from home more tolerable was likely welcome as they endured the challenging living conditions.

In *Target: Germany - The U.S. Army Air Forces' official story*

Bombs Away

of the VIII Bomber Command's first year over Europe, produced and published in London by His Majesty's Stationery Office in 1944, the general conditions of an Eighth Air Force Base are described in bleak terms: "The interminable distances on a bomber station that had to be traversed on foot with passing vehicles plastering you with freezing mud, the coal stoves in the Nissen huts that defied all attempts to keep them going overnight, the lack of hot water, the apparently permanent absence of sunlight — these things were subjects of universal lamentation and complaint, but nobody cared seriously about them. Again, it was part of fighting a war."

The men weren't there for comfort, rest or relaxation, and they acted accordingly. They mostly took the living conditions, the poor weather, mediocre food, separation from their loved ones and the constant threat of imminent death in stride...and in some cases as a hard-earned badge of honor. One can't help but wonder if being as young as most of them were helped them to cope with all of that hardship. I have little doubt that the young men fared as well as they did -- at least in part -- because they were children of the Great Depression, toughened by hard work and deprivation, and motivated by a true love of country and of their fellow soldier. Most of them weren't used to living in great comfort. I might even venture that for some of them, the living conditions and even the food could have been an improvement from what they were used to, given the tough times during the Depression.

S/Sgt. Jacob T. Elias of the 392nd Bombardment Group offered these words in *One Last Look*, by Philip Kaplan, in his later years, reflecting on life on his airbase: "Many a time, in those moments before I fall asleep, I return to that Nissen Hut. Again, we are making tea on that little stove, and there is teasing and laughing..."

"I don't want my sons to experience war. But I wish they could experience that complete camaraderie that I had at Shipdham."

Grafton-Underwood Airbase

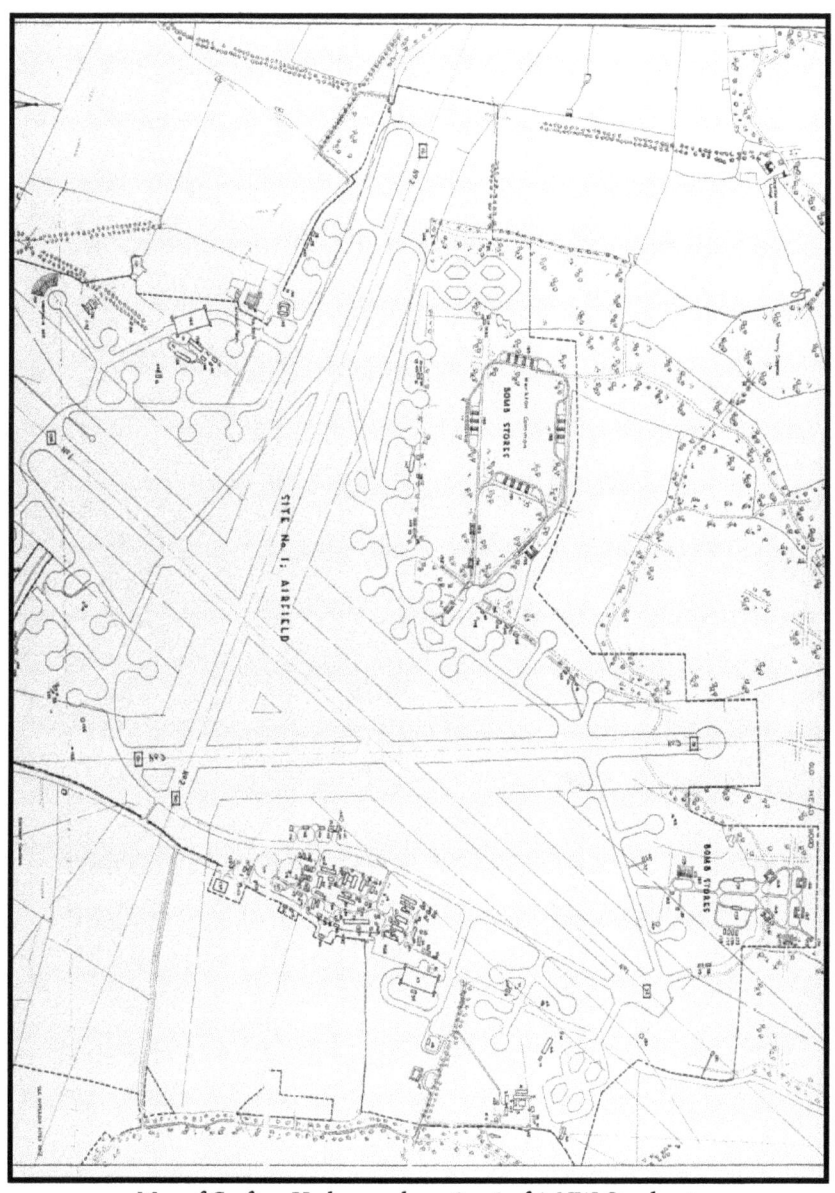

Map of Grafton-Underwood, section 1 of 4. NW Quadrant.
(Courtesy of 384thBombGroup.com)

Pro Kid

Bombs Away

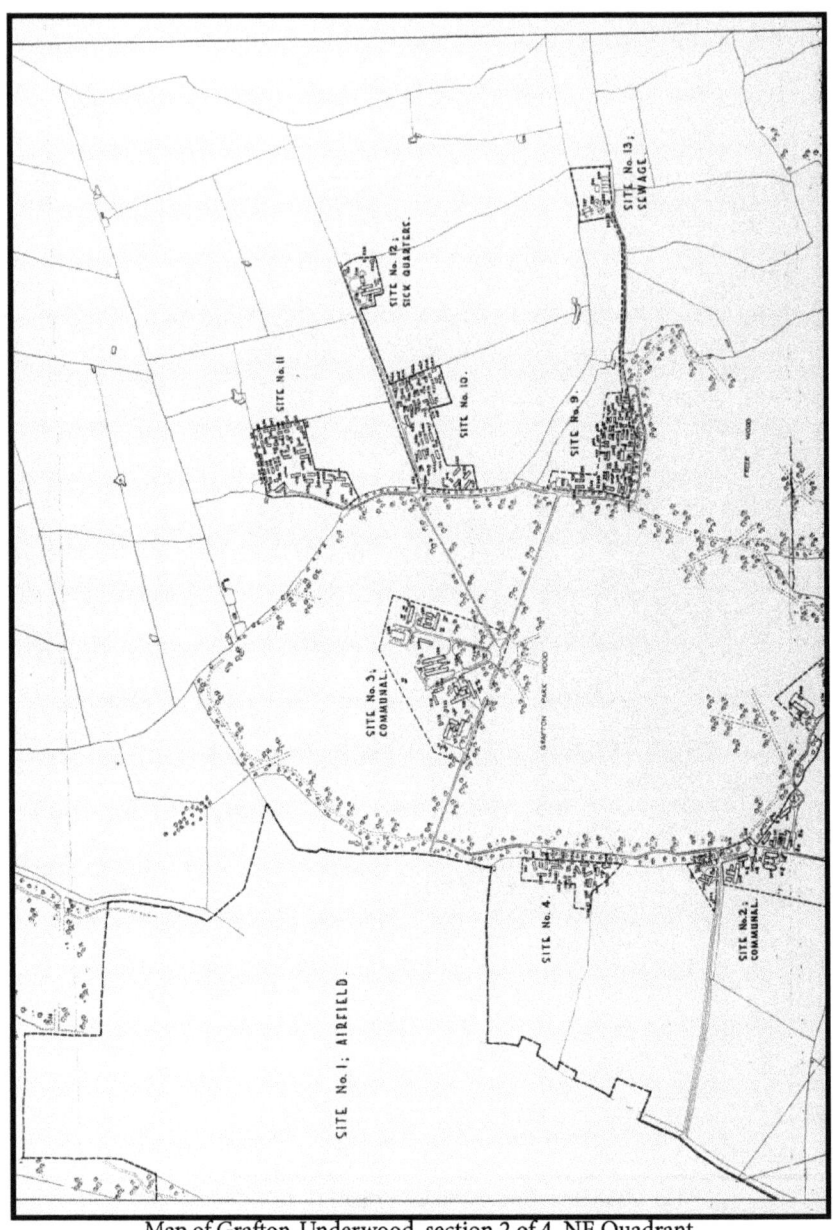

Map of Grafton-Underwood, section 2 of 4. NE Quadrant.
(Courtesy of 384thBombGroup.com)

Grafton-Underwood Airbase

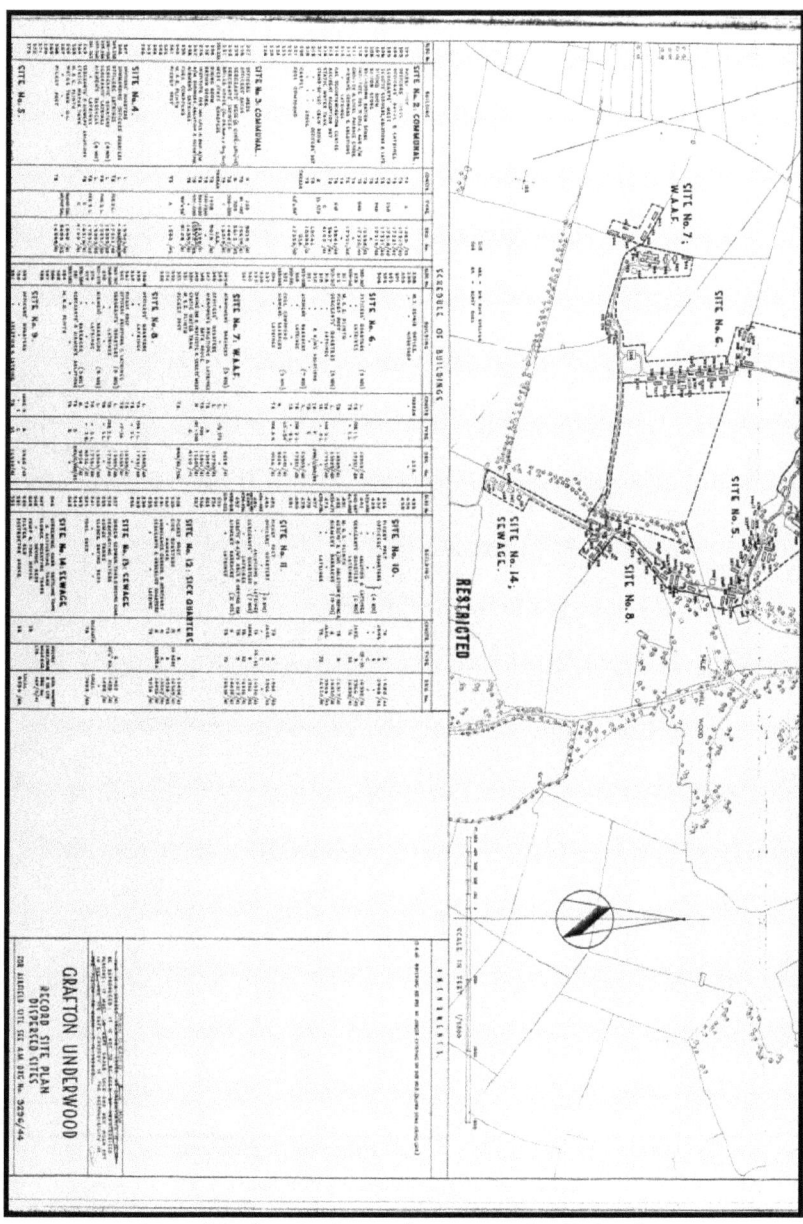

Map of Grafton-Underwood, section 4 of 4. SE Quadrant.
(Courtesy of 384thBombGroup.com)

Map of Grafton-Underwood, section 4 of 4. SE Quadrant.
(Courtesy of 384thBombGroup.com)

The Flying Fortress

4

Squinting through the ring sight of a caliber-.50 gun, down the spine of a giant Flying Fortress, right smack into the teeth of every kind of Nazi fighter plane that you can find in the recognition charts — that's when you realize why the skies of Germany's industrial targets have come to be known as "The Big League."
- John R. McCrary, in *First of the Many*

The aircraft that Herbert Small, and nearly 200,000 other airmen would be flying, or flying in, was the venerable Boeing B-17 Flying Fortress, a four-engine bomber and one of the first of its kind. In 1934, well before the war, the Army Air Corps was looking for a four-engine bomber, because most of the previous bombers had been two-engine planes, which were underpowered, and incapable of long-distance, high-altitude bombing missions. The creation of this heavy bomber marked a turning point in military aircraft.

The origins of the B-17 are discussed in *Decision Over Schwein-*

Bombs Away

furt, by Thomas M. Coffey: "The B-17 had grown directly out of the American concept of strategic daylight precision bombing. By the early thirties, Army Air Corps planners realized that, to make such a concept work, they would need the toughest, best armed, longest ranging and most complicated warplane ever devised. In 1934, they had granted the Boeing Aircraft Company a contract to develop such a plane, and the graceful, four engine Flying Fortress of 1943 was the direct descendant of the bomber Boeing undertook to design. But in nine years, so many changes had been made that only the 104-foot wingspan remained the same."

The engines were a 1200-horsepower, turbo super-charged American design which allowed the Fortress to operate at very high altitudes, above the range of most enemy anti-aircraft fire at the time… but not above the level of enemy fighter planes. By the time the B-17G — the most commonly produced model — made its way into combat, it bristled with thirteen or more .50-caliber machine guns. This heavy firepower was positioned in the nose, beneath the nose in the "chin" of the plane, on the top with the Sperry Turret and bottom of the fuselage with the Sperry Ball Turret, in the tail and along the sides or "waist" of the plane, as well. The turrets in the upper fuselage and the belly were power-operated, and the turret under the belly, or "ball turret," required an operator of small stature to be able to fit in its cramped confines.

The wingspan of the behemoth bomber was over 103 feet, and the plane was over seventy-four feet long. To put that in perspective, a usual full-sized American yellow school bus is about 40 feet long, so the B-17 was nearly double that length, and it stretched about a third of a football field in width. Its maximum speed was approximately 287 miles per hour, with a cruising speed of 182 mph, and its range exceeded 2,000 miles when carrying a full bombload of 6,000 pounds, often twelve of the standard 500-pound bombs. Unloaded, its "ferry" range was approximately 3,750 miles, which gave it more than enough range for them to be able to fly the bombers from their various bases in the United States over to the United Kingdom. Many training bases were in the western states, like California and New Mexico, as well as in Texas and Florida,

The Flying Fortress

among others, so one typical route to the U.K. was the Northern route with a stop-over in Newfoundland or Labrado, Canada before making the final "hop" over to England, where they would be put into action. That said, the trip was still not an easy one, and certainly was not one of great comforts; the B-17s were noisy, cold and the limited seating was not built for luxury.

> **[In Chapter Two, William Laubenstein describes the B-17 as being unable to make the trip across the Atlantic Ocean, but the specs for the B-17G, of which *Little Barney* was one, show that the Ferry Range of the plane was 3,750 miles. That would have been more than enough to go from somewhere in the Northeastern United States, like New York or Maine, all the way to England. I believe Laubenstein may have meant that they couldn't go all the way from Florida — the site of their last training base — to the bases in England, which would have been true. Also, the Ferry Range was for a plane carrying virtually no cargo. Usually when the B-17s were sent overseas for service, they were filled with all manner of equipment, gear and supplies for the bases they would be assigned to, with all that weight substantially reducing their range.]**

The B-17 ordinarily hosted a crew of ten men; pilot, co-pilot, navigator, bombardier (all four of whom were officers), radio operator, engineer (who also operated the top turret gun) and four men who were strictly gunners — two at the waist, one in the tail and one in the ball turret on the belly of the plane. They flew in tight formations, often of nine or twelve aircraft in groups of three, to maximize their defensive ability. Even at altitudes of 25,000 to 35,000 feet, which kept them safe from some anti-aircraft fire, they were still not safe from enemy fighters, which took an awful toll throughout the war. Losses due to enemy

Bombs Away

fighter planes in 1943 became so bad that long-distance bombing operations had to be temporarily suspended until longer-range fighters like the P-51 Mustang became available as fighter-escorts. By early 1944, the superior design, range and effectiveness of the Mustangs made them a key weapon for bomber operations based in England, and their implementation helped to turn the tide of the air war.

The interior of a B-17 was a marvel of engineering and design, featuring an impressive amount of technology to enable the men to better perform their duties. An intercom was mounted at each battle station, allowing the men to communicate throughout the plane via their headsets. Because of the high altitudes and lack of cabin pressurization, oxygen masks were required to breathe above 10,000 feet, and the men had to wear heavy sheepskin-lined coats, pants, gloves and hats, along with electrically heated suits, to keep themselves from freezing. At the higher altitudes, if a man touched any metal with his bare hands, he would stick to it. Occasionally men learned this the hard way when a combat situation required more manual dexterity than was allowed while wearing the bulky insulated gloves. They paid a high price in pain on those occasions.

There were miles of cables and wires strung throughout the plane, and most of the technology was relatively simple by today's standards. The rudders and other control surfaces were operated mostly by physical strength via the cables, and if enemy bullets or flak hit certain areas, the pilot could lose control, a radio could be knocked out or the intercom system could go quiet. There was also no standard "auto-pilot" feature in the Flying Fortress except a very rudimentary system that held a straight course while the pilot turned control over to the bombardier for the bombing run. This meant that an eight- or ten-hour flight would require someone to have his hands on the controls at all times, making for a very strenuous flying experience, especially in times when the planes were damaged, and the pilots were struggling to keep them aloft and flying straight.

There were few creature comforts on the B-17, regardless of

The Flying Fortress

which model they were flying, but because the temperatures could reach well below freezing, the crew could plug into an electric heating system that warmed special suits lined with heating coils. Unfortunately, sometimes heavy exertion would cause the men to sweat under their heavy clothes, which meant they would sometimes receive tiny electric shocks when parts of the suits shorted out. It was a common nuisance for the men, but something they endured; it was better than frostbite! The main oxygen system throughout the plane at each battle station allowed each man to breathe at the high altitudes, and scattered about were also small, portable oxygen bottles, which enabled the men to move around while still being able to breathe comfortably. These could also be used in an emergency if a crew-member's individual oxygen supply was compromised somehow.

According to R.J. Overy in *The Bombers and the Bombed*, "The Eighth Air Force crews had some advantages compared to crews aboard other types of bombers; the B-17 Flying Fortress was less cold to fly in, and they were provided with good thermal clothing; each aircraft had a pilot and copilot; attacking aircraft were more easily visible, though the limited range of the B-17 machine guns meant that rocket- and cannon-firing fighters could damage the bombers before facing risk themselves."

Serving in a B-17 Flying Fortress shared very little in common with the commercial flying experience of the average person these days. It was often hot on the ground as they waited for take-off, cold and loud in the air and dangerous any time they were flying, especially during forming up and when enemy aircraft were attacking. When not engaged with the enemy, there was still plenty of danger from mechanical malfunctions, human error, bad weather or a hundred other things that could go wrong. Many a crew was turned back to base because an engine's supercharger or turbo was not functioning properly…or some other system on the plane failed. Flying in those days was certainly not an easy task.

Idiot's Delight

Bombs Away

[A 'supercharger' was a device fitted to each engine on the B-17 which used the engine exhaust gas to increase horsepower by passing it through an ingenious series of mechanisms. The various steps in the chain heat the gas, increase the pressure and eventually cool it back down. I won't do it justice in my own words, so here is how it's described on "www.airpages.ru:"

"Each engine on the B-17 has a turbo-supercharger which boosts manifold pressure for take-off and provides sea-level air pressure at high altitudes. To operate the turbo-superchargers, engine exhaust gas passes through the collector ring and tail-stack to the nozzle, and drives the bucket wheel at high speed.

"A ramming air inlet duct from the leading edge of the wing supplies air to the impeller, which increases pressure and temperature. However, in order to avoid detonation at the carburetor, the air supplied to the carburetor passes through the intercooler, where the temperature is reduced. The internal engine impeller, driven by the engine crankshaft, again increases air pressure as it enters the intake manifold. Higher intake manifold pressure results in greater power output."

Did you get all that?!]

From *First of the Many*, the incredible book by John R. McCrary, a photographer who flew with the Eighth Air Force, the author wrote in a letter to his brother Lt. Douglas A. McCrary, Navy: "There are so damn many ways to get killed in a Fortress, special ways: your oxygen mask can freeze up and you'll keel over before you can get help or yell for it, and you're a stiff in ten minutes; you can get fragments of flak or 20mm shells…both will make a mess out of you; you can get hit by

The Flying Fortress

rocket projectiles or air-to-air bombing; or you can crash head-on with a Focke-Wulf; any one of four engines or several gas tanks can stop an explosive slug; or maybe a couple of your engines go out, and you lag behind the formation, and then the fighters cut you to pieces."

[The first edition of *First of the Many* was actually published in 1944! Yeah, while the war was still going on! I was able to find a copy in my local St. Louis library system, and it was like holding a piece of living history.]

*****

Taking a tour of the B-17, if we enter the plane from the rear access hatch, then move left toward the tail, we find the Tail Gunner, who operated twin .50-caliber Browning machine guns, which were supplied

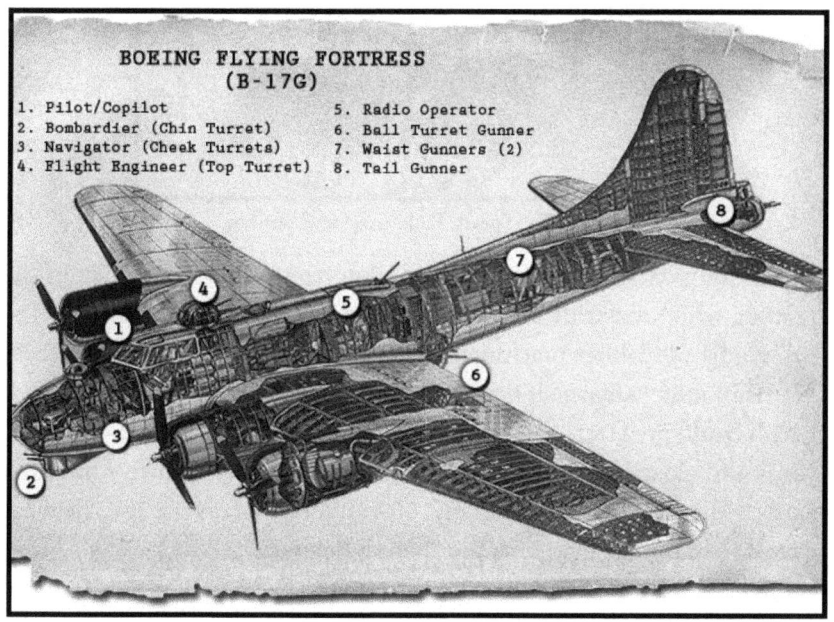

BOEING FLYING FORTRESS (B-17G)
1. Pilot/Copilot
2. Bombardier (Chin Turret)
3. Navigator (Cheek Turrets)
4. Flight Engineer (Top Turret)
5. Radio Operator
6. Ball Turret Gunner
7. Waist Gunners (2)
8. Tail Gunner

The positions on a B-17G. (Courtesy of Sarah Sundin Books.)

Bombs Away

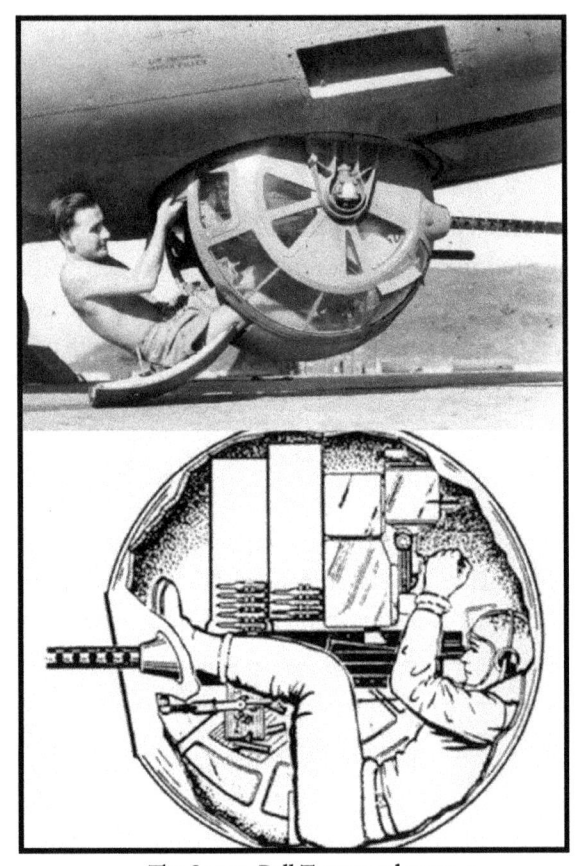

The Sperry Ball Turret and gunner.

with hundreds of rounds by two wooden troughs on either side of the gunner, who sat astride an infamously uncomfortable bicycle seat. The Browning .50-caliber machine gun was a staple of armament in World War II in many arenas. It fired a round that was nearly a half-inch thick which could penetrate steel armor plating nearly an inch thick from 100 yards and close to three-quarters of an inch thick at over five hundred yards. The presence of the many .50-caliber guns on the B-17 is what gave it the famous nickname the "Flying Fortress."

The tail gunner had connections to the intercom, heating and oxygen systems on the walls on either side of him, and was protected by various levels of armor plating, depending on the particular model type

The Flying Fortress

of B-17 in which he was flying, the B-17G being the most common model produced. He would have also had, as all of the crew had, a parachute sitting very close by in the event that an evacuation from a damaged plane became necessary. The parachutes, when considered along with all of the other clothing they were wearing, were too bulky for many of them to wear while they were manning their positions, so they kept them nearby and could quickly clip them onto a harness they wore when the time came to bail out.

Moving forward from the tail, we pass by the two Waist (or Flex) Gunners, whose guns were staggered in the later B-17G model to keep the two men from constantly bumping into each other, as in earlier models when they were placed side-by-side. This staggered set-up was good for mobility and defensive capabilities, but it left the two gunners vulnerable from behind, because the armor plating was not extended in the later models due to weight concerns. A nuisance and hazard for the waist gunners was the piling up of the spent bullet casings around their feet on the floor, which necessitated the shuffling of their feet to change position, rather than lifting their feet and risking uncertain footing. The waist gunners also were the coldest on the B-17, since their guns were mounted in open slots on the sides of the planes, with nothing to shield them from the freezing winds blasting in.

Next up we find the Ball Turret Gunner, located on the belly of the plane, just in front of the Waist Gunners. His turret could be entered from outside the plane or inside it, through a small hatch, by rotating the turret to where the guns pointed straight down. The turret was operated hydraulically by pedals the gunner worked with his feet, allowing a 360-degree field of fire...everywhere but up, of course. The diminutive ball gunner would often be stuck in the cramped space for hours with very little ability to move about or stretch...or to answer the call of nature. Many ball turret gunners devised ingenious contraptions to allow themselves to urinate during the long hours they spent manning their guns.

There are a few reported cases of B-17s suffering severe damage to the landing gear as well as to the mechanisms operating the ball turrets. On these occasions, if they were not able to pivot the turret into position to allow for the gunner to get out, he would be stuck. He would be forced to remain in his turret while the plane made a very dangerous belly landing, tragically crushing the gunner under the weight of the aircraft. The ball gunner was also one of the men who could not wear his parachute while he was manning his weapon, because the space was too cramped to allow for it. He did have a safety harness that was attached to the plane in the event that the turret was shot out or came unattached, but in a bail-out situation he would have to scramble up and out as quickly as possible, find his chute and head for an exit.

> **[The ball turret gunner had to be a very rare breed of man, capable of withstanding long hours in a horribly confining and cramped space, impervious to fear of heights and claustrophobia. I wonder if I could have endured either of those conditions, much less both at once.]**

In front of the ball turret sat the Radio Operator, with a large array of communications equipment, along with a small lamp and desk for writing. His main job was to communicate with the other Fortresses or the base if in range, but his duties also included taking position reports every thirty minutes and assisting with navigation. The Radio Operator was also expected to fire a single .50-caliber machine gun that was located on the top of the plane midway between the waist gunners and the top turret. How these planes didn't wind up cutting each other to pieces with their own crossfire is hard to imagine, but somehow they managed. The number of guns that would have been firing, multiplied by the number of aircraft in formation must have made for an absolute maelstrom of fire.

From the radio room, we move forward to the twin bomb bays, which were stacked with bombs all the way to the top of the fuselage and traversed by a very narrow catwalk for those moving forward or aft. A full bomb load was 6,000 pounds, made up of anywhere from

The Flying Fortress

A good look at the Chin Turret and Top Turret on *Big Stupe V*.
(Courtesy of 384thBombGroup.com

100-pound munitions to the largest 500-pound bombs; the bombload varied based on the type of mission the Group was tasked with, and the bombs would be meticulously loaded by the ground crews typically in the early hours of the morning while the aircrews were at their briefings learning about the mission.

In the adjoining space moving forward from the bomb bays we find the main oxygen tanks and hydraulic systems, as well as the ladder up to the cockpit and rotating top turret. This space housed the Flight Engineer, who also operated the top Sperry Turret of twin .50-caliber machine guns. He would have the upper version counterpart of the ball turret 360-degree view from his post and would be a pivotal defensive position in the plane, especially when attacked from above, which was a common Luftwaffe tactic. His main job (while not on the gun) was to monitor the plane's various systems…oxygen, hydraulics, electrical…

Cockpit of a B-17. Pilot on the left, co-pilot on the right.   (Stock photo.)

and make adjustments or repairs as needed. He was a "Jack of all trades" who would be called upon to fix anything that could go wrong on such a complicated machine. And there was a lot that could go wrong.

Very little was operated by hydraulics throughout the plane, with the thought being that if there were hydraulic lines running everywhere, damage to them could disable the entire plane. Electrical systems were also run separately in many cases, to avoid a single bit of damage causing a total outage. An immense amount of thought, design and planning went into the building of the B-17, and the ground crews were constantly making modifications and upgrades of their own, both of the officially endorsed variety and otherwise, to improve performance.

From the engineer's space, we could climb up to the cockpit, shared by the Pilot and Co-Pilot, with all of the dials and switches that operated the various flight systems, or go forward underneath the cock-

The Flying Fortress

pit into the Navigator and Bombardier spaces. In the cockpit, in front of and between the two seats…pilot on the left, co-pilot on the right…were the throttles, fuel mixture controls, landing gear controls and numerous dials, switches and gauges for everything from airspeed and altitude to the tachometer and voltmeter; and of course, the twin steering yolks for the pilot and co-pilot. Compared to modern technology, 1940s flight technology seems rather primitive, but the men had all they needed to operate the plane properly.

Underneath and forward of the cockpit was the space for the Navigator in the nose of the plane. He had a desk and chair, like the radio operator, and various radio and navigational devices crucial to keeping the Ship on course. The navigator would also operate the twin "cheek" guns; individual .50-caliber machine guns located on either side of the navigator/bombardier compartment, adding extra firepower to the mix when needed. If there was an additional navigator, as was the case when Col. Dale Smith implemented his policy of the lead plane

View of the Bombardier's position. The Norden Bombsight is in the middle, controls for the chin turret are on the upper right and the ammunition feeds for the cheeck guns are on either side and the floor. (Stock photo.)

Deuces Wild

Bombs Away

using two navigators, each man could fire one of the cheek guns, when necessary.

The Bombardier was set up in the very front of the plexiglass nose, where he had his cherished and Top-Secret Norden Bomb Sight, as well as the remote controls for the twin .50-caliber machine guns in the "chin-turret" that sat directly below his position. The Norden Bomb Sight was an ingenious device that could measure the plane's ground speed and direction, among other factors, much more accurately than earlier devices, which made for much more accurate bombing. It was a big advancement for its time and is believed to have been a decisive factor in the success of the bombing campaigns.

The chin-turret was a later addition in the B-17G that had a huge impact on aircraft defense, because prior to its introduction, none of the guns on the Fort could actually fire straight ahead, making the head-on attack a very popular and successful tactic of the Luftwaffe fighters. Even the ball turret and top gun were not able to fire straight ahead and

Two ground crewmen take a break for a photo.
(Courtesy of 384thBombGroup.com)

The Flying Fortress

at either a slightly upward or downward angle to be able to effectively thwart head-on attacks, which became a staple for the Luftwaffe once the vulnerability was discovered. Some were critical of the addition of the chin turret because it reportedly slowed the plane's top speed down by about ten miles per hour, but most of the airmen seemed glad to have the extra firepower and to close the gaping hole in their field of fire.

The way the B-17 Bomber Groups were arranged while in formation was designed to maximize the defensive ability of the .50-caliber guns on all of the aircraft combined, each individual Fort being able to help cover numerous others in their vicinity. Despite the heavy advantage in speed and maneuverability on the part of the enemy fighters compared to the bombers, when flying in a tight defensive formation, the B-17s put up a very formidable defense from those hundreds of guns firing in all directions. A formation would usually be made up of small clusters of three aircraft arranged in a "V" formation (also known as the "V of Vs"), with an individual Group being made up of three or four of the small three-plane clusters. Three such Groups — Lead Group, High Group and Low Group — would compose a Wing, which could include as many as fifty-four aircraft, known as the Combat Box, a concept that is credited to Col. Curtis E. LeMay. The very last ship in the Low Group would be the last in the entire formation and bore the morbid nicknames Tail-End Charlie and Purple Heart Corner, because of the high vulnerability of the position.

No discussion of the B-17 Flying Fortress, or the Eighth Air Force as a whole, is complete without a strong mention of the ground crews that worked on these storied aircraft. The mere act of getting dozens of planes ready for each mission required numerous pieces of preparation to be accomplished, regardless of weather. Each plane had to be outfitted with the proper amount of fuel for the specific mission — it wasn't just a standard amount that was used each time they took off. Nearly 7,000 rounds of .50-caliber machine gun ammunition would have to be loaded in position for the various guns, and sometimes as much as 11,000 rounds, depending on the mission. The typical load for each gun was

Bombs Away

1,460 rounds for the chin turret, 800 rounds for the upper turret, 200 rounds for the single .50-cal. used by the radio operator, 1,000 rounds for the ball turret, 1,200 for each of the two waist gunners and 1,130 for the tail gunner. Additional rounds were supplied to the cheek guns, as well.

The oxygen system had to be filled and checked to make sure it was fully functional. The heating system for the warming suits had to be working properly or the men would likely not survive the extreme temperatures. The bomb load had to be established and loaded into the bomb bays, and every other system on the plane had to be checked to ensure it was in proper working order. And all that was expected when the planes were not also damaged and in need of repair.

Often these tough and durable planes were brought back to base in such a state of damage that those who witnessed their return were amazed the planes could even remain aloft, much less be flown hun-

Another dedicated ground crew toils on an engine repair.
(Courtesy of 384thBombGroup.com).

The Flying Fortress

dreds of miles back to base. Damaged planes were quickly assessed by ground crews as to whether they were salvageable or if they were destined for the parts depot, where they would be slowly picked apart in service of repairing and maintaining the aircraft that were still capable of being sent into battle. Those that were salvageable were worked on tirelessly for as long as it took to get them back in the fight.

The ground crews performed near miracles in getting damaged aircraft back into fighting shape. Parts were stripped off of other planes too far gone to save, then welded, riveted or screwed back onto the planes that needed them, and much of it was done in an astoundingly short time, while enduring horrible weather conditions. These men were the true unsung "heroes behind the heroes" of the 8th Air Force.

Roger Freeman, in *The Mighty Eighth War Manual*, had much to say about the ground crews; "For every combatant in [the] 8th Air Force, there were 20 personnel in a supporting ground role." "Each bomber had two ground mechanics assigned, a Crew Chief and an Assistant Crew Chief. These two administered the same aircraft and it became 'their' plane far more than the aircrew's who flew it." "The armorer was the third member of the ground crew team, usually assigned to one aircraft but sometimes having to serve two. He was the first member of the ground crew at the aircraft, and most armorers tried to steal some sleep in the tent before the crew chief arrived by cycle to carry out pre-flight check."

To give an idea of the scope of what was involved behind the scenes by the ground crews in putting a full complement of bombers into the air for some of the bigger missions, I'll turn to a publication put out in 1944 by the Army Air Forces in London, printed by "His Majesty's Stationery Office titled *Target: Germany: The U.S. Army Air Forces' Official Story of the the VIII Bomber Command's First Year Over Europe:* "If 500 American heavy bombers attack a group of enemy targets, they will ordinarily represent less than half the total operational force at the Command's disposal — approximately 750 bombers being held either in reserve or under repair. Each of these 1250 bombers has its combat crew of ten men and its ground crew of five mechanics. Each station participating in the attack also has its corps of specialists — radio experts, armorers, refueling teams, ordnance and armament men and engineering officers — who work directly on the flying equipment. This specialist group, for a force of 1250 planes, might represent another 24,000 officers and men. Thus the 500 bombers over the target are immediately dependent on an army of more than 30,000 highly trained specialists."

Not only did the Grafton-Underwood men — and likely those at all Eighth Air Force bases — show their ingenuity in improving their living conditions. They also displayed an incredible amount of it in the way they worked on the B-17s. In *As Briefed*, Walter Owens makes specific reference to how the men on the ground crews were constantly innovating and improving to make their jobs easier. "…hundreds of Grafton-Underwood men made their own little contributions. It might be a simple screwdriver so shaped that it would enable a mechanic to remove one damaged part without disassembling the entire piece of machinery. It might be a new tool to meet one specific problem. It might be a hoist or a stand or a cart that would speed up the time required to do a routine job. It might be anything, but if the need was there someone would find the answer."

Without the ground crews, the task would have been impossible — a non-starter. Without their incredible dedication, devotion to their planes and the crews that flew them, and the absolute mastery of their craft, the effectiveness and outcome of the bombing campaign would have been very different. In all of my research, I have yet to find one ill word spoken of those who worked on the planes on the ground.

Arriving in October of 1943, and not flying his first mission until mid-November that year, meant that Herb missed being part of one of the worst times of the war for the Eighth Air Force. Losses to planes and men were very heavy towards the end of 1942, such that by the first few weeks of 1943, some Bomber Groups had lost nearly eighty percent of their original crews. Losses continued through the fall of 1943, with the 384th alone losing seventeen crews during the months of September and October, one to a non-combat accident and sixteen others on missions.

The Flying Fortress

One of the main problems the bomber crews faced was the lack of sufficient support from fighters. The American fighters being used primarily to that point in the European theater were the P-38 Lightning, which Luftwaffe pilots referred to as "the fork-tailed devil" due to its unusual dual-airframe design, and the P-47 Thunderbolt. Both were good airplanes, loved by those who flew them, and always a welcome sight to bombers crews. However, the P-38s were not maneuverable enough to compete well with the German Focke-Wulf 190 and Messerschmitt 109, which were both faster and more agile. The P-47s were more capable of matching the German fighters, but they lacked sufficient fuel range to be effective on anything but the shorter missions until 1944 when auxiliary "drop-tanks" were added to increase their range. Before that, German pilots needed only to wait for the bombers to outfly their fighter escorts' range and then start their attacks, with only the bombers' guns to fend them off.

Originally, U.S. military leadership believed that the incredible amount of defensive firepower put out by the bomber groups while in their tightly packed formation would be more than enough to protect them. Unfortunately, they had to learn the hard way the massive advantage the fast-moving, highly maneuverable fighters had over the lumbering bombers. The thin aluminum outer shell of the B-17 offered virtually no protection against enemy bullets or anti-aircraft "flak," which was an anti-aircraft defense used by the Germans against aerial bombardment; the term was an abbreviation of the German word "*fliegerabwehrkanone,*" that means "aircraft defense cannon." There were as many as 10,000 German anti-aircraft artillery pieces and an estimated 900,000 men operating them throughout different stages of the homeland defense of Germany and its occupied territory. A well-trained anti-aircraft team could fire up to twenty rounds per minute and the shells could be set to explode at a specific height, depending on the altitude at which the enemy fighters were flying. When the shells blew up, they sprayed jagged pieces of metal shrapnel in all directions, tearing through the thin-skinned planes and shredding the flesh of the men.

Certain areas of the B-17 were armored, including parts of the cockpit and parts of the fuselage protecting the oxygen system, plus there was some armor plating giving limited protection to the various gunners. But it was all about weight, and there were trade-offs that had to be made to keep from taking too much capacity away from the bombload by investing more weight in armor. The glass in some parts of the planes was bullet-resistant, and would also offer some protection, but not against direct hits from the cannons of the Messerschmitts or the Focke-Wulfs.

The men also wore 30-pound flak-suits and steel helmets, which were heavy and cumbersome, but offered some additional protection against flying shrapnel and debris. The flak-suits even helped somewhat in keeping the men warm in the severe temperatures at high altitudes, but they could be removed quickly by pulling a ripcord if the men needed to bail out in an emergency. The suits were too bulky to allow the men to also wear their parachutes, so those were kept nearby and donned quickly, often on the way out of a doomed ship.

By the latter part of 1943, the heavy losses became so bad that the number of missions was temporarily reduced, partly by necessity, because it took time to resupply the bases with both airships and men to fly them, and partly because the military leaders were reevaluating their bomber strategies. Thankfully, the tide was about to turn in the Allies' favor with the timely introduction of the P-51 Mustang into the war in early 1944.

One can only imagine the level of stress and fear these men experienced before, during and after every mission. Flying at altitudes of up to 30,000 feet, in temperatures down to negative fifty degrees Fahrenheit, with enemy fighters trying to shoot them down as they returned fire from deafening machine guns all around them. Have you ever wondered why so many of the older men we knew while growing up were hard of hearing? Our uncles, fathers or grandfathers? If they were veterans, it was very likely because they fought on the ground, in the air or on the ocean with only a minimal concept of the damage to their hearing that they were enduring on a daily basis from the deafening blasts of rifles,

The Flying Fortress

machine guns, cannons and other explosions. Men often tried to wad up balls of cloth, paper, cotton or whatever else they could find, but it was usually insufficient to provide real protection for their ears.

One very popular practice among the men that was probably not in any of the Boeing or Army Air Force operations manuals was that of decorating the nose of the bombers, especially the B-17 Flying Fortresses and B-24 Liberators. "Nose Art," often depicting female movie stars and "Pin-Up Girls" of the day — such as Marlene Dietrich, Doris Day and Rita Hayworth — was very popular. Generic cartoon beauties were also often shown in various stages of undress, to the delight and amusement of the airmen, with risqué names to go along with the pictures, like *Sexy Suzy* and *Virgin on the Verge*. Nose Art also featured cartoon

The one-of-a-kind *Spotted Cow*. (Courtesy of 384thBombGroup.com.)

drawings with names that sometimes contained ominous or threatening messages for the enemy, such as *Dynamite Express, Hell's Messenger* or *Pistol Packin' Mama.*

The practice of naming the aircraft rivaled the Nose Art in popularity and creativity. It was often inspired by the love of a special girl, the fighting spirit of the men or their quirky sense of humor...sometimes all rolled into one. Names like *Memphis Belle, Yankee Lady* and *Susan Ruth** were endearing tributes to sweethearts back home. *Reno's Raider,*

Bombs Away

Rain of Terror and *Dynamite Express* were meant to strike fear into the hearts of the enemy, while *Phartzac, Nuttall's Nut House* and *Idiots Delight* showed the men's efforts, sometimes admittedly juvenile, to lighten things up a bit.

> **[I can very easily imagine these young but grown men…these warriors…giggling like schoolboys when their dignified and stoic commanding officers were forced to recite names like *Phartzac, Ex-Virgin* and *Little Willie* over their radios or intercoms. I'm 52 and I know it would crack me up a little!]**

> **[*Steve Snyder, author and son of 1st Lt. Howard J. Snyder, wrote an excellent book titled "Shot Down: The true story of pilot Howard Snyder and the crew of the B-17 *Susan Ruth*." It is a very good read and worth checking out.]**

There was also the slightly more off-color side of the names, as the men made great use of innuendo to give us a clue what else was on their minds a good portion of the time; *Vertical Shaft, Hard to Get, Randie Lou, Satan's Sister* and *Sweater Girl*, just to name a few. In the stories and our collective imaginings, these men have in many cases become larger-than-life heroes, but we must not forget that they were only human, and in the end, boys will be boys.

These men were indeed a different breed. Despite their lighter side and all the hardship of war, once they were up in the air, it was all business. Somehow, despite the lack of sleep, challenging living conditions and all of the chaos of a bombing mission, they were able to focus on the task at hand. They did their jobs as they were trained, bravely and with purpose, knowing that they may be wounded, shot down or killed at any moment. They largely volunteered for this duty and trained long and hard to execute their missions properly when called upon to do so.

The Flying Fortress

Base Commander Col. Dale O. Smith had this to say on the subject of fear in his memoirs *Screaming Eagle: Memoirs of a B-17 Group Commander*: "One's mind simply cannot attend to more than one subject of concentration at the same time. So, if I didn't think of the danger, the fear diminished. Moreover, familiarity with the danger, after I survived a number of missions, tended to give me the fatalism I needed — that sense of living a charmed life. If I took all necessary precautions and drilled my group in flying a tight defensive formation while emphasizing gunnery training, then whatever happened was in the hands of the gods." He also added, "…to blanket fear, keep busy."

Twin brothers, S/SSgts. Richard and Robert Egger of the 547th Bomb Squadron posing at the tail gun. (Courtesy of 384thBombGroup.com)

Bombs Away

Pistol Packin Mamma (Courtesy of 384thBombGroup.com)

Dynamite Express (Courtesy of 384thBombGroup.com)

The Flying Fortress

Snuffy (Courtesy of 384thBombGroup.com)

Stella. Notice Lt. John Curtin's name at his navigator's window. (Courtesy of 384thBombGroup.com)

Bombs Away

B-17G Aces and Ates. (Courtesy of 384thBombGroup.com)

The Crew

5

"When the pressure is greatest, there among the people fighting on our side, you will find the most heroes."

-John R. McCrary, *First of the Many*

Herbert Small was assigned to the 384th Bomber Group, along with his crew, by way of Army Air Force Station 106 Special Orders #136, effective November 5, 1943. All of his original flight crew, with the exception of 2nd Lt. Earl Allison, were assigned to the 384th via that same Special Order effective the same date of November 5th. Curiously, Earl Allison was assigned with an effective date of October 5, 1943, but he didn't fly his first mission until November 26, 1943, ten days after Herb flew his first mission with an entirely different crew.

I don't know the reason for such a long delay for Allison before his first mission; it could have been weather issues, personnel issues or even something mechanical having to do with the aircraft on the ground.

Bombs Away

Whatever the reason, by right around Thanksgiving 1943, he was in the action and fighting, putting to use all of his training of the previous year.

The crew that Herb flew his first two missions with was made up of:

- Capt. Randolph G. E. Jacobs — Pilot.
- 2nd Lt. Herbert W. Small — Co-Pilot
- 2nd Lt. John Q. Curtin — Navigator
- Lt. David H. Davis — Bombardier
- Pvt. Victor H. Duro — Radio Operator
- Staff Sgt. Jack K. Goetz — Engineer/Top Turret
- Sgt. Donald F. Gorham — Ball Turret Gunner
- Staff Sgt. Robert L. Compton — Tail Gunner
- Tech Sgt. Aldo J. Gregori — Waist Gunner
- Staff Sgt. Lawrence H. Wager — Waist Gunner

Of special note to remember for later in Herb's story are Capt. Randolph Jacobs (also known as "Jake," "Moose" or "Randy") and 2nd Lt. John Curtin, with whom Herb flew only two missions and one mission respectively. By November 16, 1943, Capt. Jacobs had nine completed missions already under his belt, having also started an additional eight missions that were aborted due to various complications, mechanical problems or weather-related issues after take-off. He had been up in the air seventeen times to that point, with nine missions in the books.

Often the new pilots were paired with more seasoned pilots to get them some critical mission experience, which is why Herb was flying with Jacobs; the same thing was done with navigators, which is why Herb's usual navigator 2nd Lt. Sam Gardner flew his first mission (also on November 16th) with a completely different crew than what was his usual assigned crew. The responsibility of forming up at the beginning of a mission and then following the flight plan was a heavy one for the pilot and navigator, in particular, and any hands-on wartime experience they could gain from those who had already been on missions was in-

The Crew

valuable.

As for the remaining seven guys who were on the crew from Herb's first mission, Herb flew two missions with each of them, and three missions total with one: waist gunner Lawrence H. Wager. The Randolph Jacobs crew was a very prolific and successful crew, with some of the guys flying as many as thirty-five missions with Capt. Jacobs. They were given the added responsibility of helping to train newly arrived pilots to help get them up to speed. Starting with that November 16th mission, Capt. Jacobs had several different co-pilots over the next few months, helping to get the new men some hours in the air with a seasoned team.

In *As Briefed*, Capt. Walter Owens tells an incredible story about Jacobs that shows us exactly why the new pilots and crews were excited to fly with him. On his third mission, on August 17, 1943, Jacobs and crew were part of a mission to bomb a ball bearing factory in Schweinfurt, Germany, a city that saw a lot of attention from the Eighth Air Force. During the mission aboard *El Rauncho*, Jacobs and crew experienced heavy battle damage and were forced to crash land back at Grafton-Underwood. Owens recalls, "The *El Rauncho* pointed steeply down, then leveled off at the treetops and began feeling for the runway. She must have been going a hundred and fifty miles an hour when the friction of aluminum on concrete began throwing off sparks. The plane slid at a terrific pace the full length of the runway, screeching all the

El Rauncho after its crash landing. (Courtesy of 384thBombGroup.com)

Bombs Away

way and leaving a shower of sparks behind. At the far end she whirled abruptly about and careened over an anti-aircraft emplacement, finally coming to a stop only twenty-five yards from a parked aircraft.

"The crowd of ground men surged forward, but by the time the first one got there, Jacobs had already pried himself loose and was calmly shoving a cigar in his mouth.

"*'Anybody got a light,'* he was saying, *'We didn't have enough gasoline left to fill our cigarette lighters.'*"

That's the kind of pilot Randolph Jacobs was.

The original crew of *Little Barney*. L-to-R Back: Earl Allison (P), Jack Nagel (B), Sam Gardner (N), Herbert Small (CP), L-to-R Front: Kenneth Hougard (T), Vernon Kaufman (BT), James Grimmett (W/F), William Clements (E/TT), William Laubenstein (R), [William Kouski is absent from this picture for unknown reasons.] (Courtesy of 384thBombGroup.com)

The Crew

*****

It wasn't until Herb's third mission, nearly a month later on December 13th, that he was reunited with what would be his regular crew, with occasional subs, for the remainder of his missions. Four of Herb's missions were aborted; three for mechanical problems and one because the entire group had difficulty forming up after take-off due to heavy cloud cover over the area. If a mission was aborted, the men were not awarded Combat Mission Credit, so even though he went up twenty-seven times, he only received credit for twenty-three missions.

Sioux City Army Airbase. (Photo from *Sioux City Journal.*)

Herb's "regular" crew — the crew composition when he was assigned to the 384th Bomber Group as a Replacement Combat Crew and the crew he trained with back in the States — was the following:

Bombs Away

- 2nd Lt. Earl T. Allison — Pilot
- 2nd Lt. Herbert W. Small — Co-Pilot
- 2nd Lt. Sam Gardner — Navigator
- 2nd Lt. Jack C. Nagel — Bombardier
- Tech. Sgt. William F. Laubenstein — Radio Operator
- Staff Sgt. William A. Clements — Engineer/Top Turret
- Staff Sgt. Vernon H. Kaufman — Ball Turret Gunner
- Staff Sgt. Kenneth N. Hougard — Tail/Flex Gunner
- Staff Sgt. William L. Kouski — Waist/Flex Gunner
- Staff Sgt. James H. Grimmett — Waist/Flex Gunner

Lt. Earl Thomas Allison — pilot — was a fellow Massachusetts guy, which probably endeared him even more to Herb Small, though they were from entirely different ends of the state. Allison was from Beverly, Massachusetts, about fifteen miles northeast of Boston on the North Shore, as it's called, near Salem and Peabody, Mass., and just about as far from Sheffield as you can be and still be in Massachusetts.

[And that's NOT pronounced "Pea Body," mind you. It's "Peabitty." Don't get me started on Quincy, Gloucester or Worcester.]

He enlisted in Boston on March 27th, 1942, and did part of his training at Wendover Airfield in Utah on the border with Nevada near the famous Bonneville Salt Flats, then moved on to the Sioux City Air Base in northwest Iowa. Wendover was activated as an Army Air Base on March 28, 1942, for B-17 and B-24 heavy bombardment training and began receiving trainees and squadrons of B-17s in mid-April 1942. In all, there were twenty-one bomber groups and more than 1,000 aircrews — roughly 10,000 men — that completed training at Wendover Air Base. Eventually, training for bombardment groups ended in April 1944 when they switched over to training P-47 fighter pilots.

Elements of the 384th Bomb Group and the 544th Bomb Squadron trained at Wendover, along with twenty other Bomb Groups, in-

The Crew

Earl Allison with his bike and in his Mae West life jacket.
(Photos courtesy of 384thBombGroup.com

cluding the 100th Bomb Group — "The Bloody Hundredth" of recent notoriety from the excellent Apple Plus tv series *Masters of the Air*.

One source reported that when Earl Allison's training was completed, he made his way back across the country by rail and then sailed to England on the famed Queen Elizabeth cruise liner. However, I don't believe that to be the case, because William Laubenstein's memoirs very clearly describe Earl Allison as part of the crew flying *Little Barney* from their last training location in Florida over to England via Labrador and Iceland.

He was assigned to the 384th Bomb Group on November 5, 1943, the same day as Herb Small and the rest of their regular crew, but with the backdated October 5th effective date. I believe that Herb Small knew, or at least knew of, Earl Allison, before he went off to training, possibly having met him while he was studying at McLean Hospital in Belmont, MA, just west of downtown Boston, and not far from Allison's home in Beverly. It's possible they became friends on the long train ride west from Boston to California or during some phase of training. However it was that they knew each other, Herb made specific mention to

Bombs Away

his family during his early training days that he very much wanted to fly with Earl Allison. Earl was reportedly an excellent pilot and Herb felt very comfortable and confident flying with him. The two became good friends, so much so that they eventually made an agreement to notify each other's families if either was Killed in Action, via the use of a special written code in their letters back home. If a letter to the other man's mother contained all of the agreed upon words, it meant that the worst had happened. Of course, that agreement assumed that both men didn't meet the same fate at the same time, which was of a high likelihood, seeing as how they sat just a few feet away from each other on most of their missions.

There are many stories similar to this one in war...men who are close to one another agreeing to get word to the other man's family or sweetheart if something happens to him. In some cases, men agreed to gather a buddy's personal items — a cherished good luck charm, photo, bible or other item — and make sure they were returned to the family. It comforted men to know that someone was looking out for them in that way, and that they could provide the same service to their buddy, if it was the other guy who got killed.

Herb flew twenty-four missions with Earl Allison, all of them with Earl as the pilot and Herb as the co-pilot. There is no way those two men, both from Massachusetts, didn't develop a strong bond of friendship and camaraderie during the long, grueling hours and the incredibly high stress conditions under which they lived, both in the air and on the ground. The cockpit of a B-17 is not big enough for much to be hidden from the guy flying next to you for all those hours in the air.

Navigator 2nd Lt. Sam Gardner trained with Herb and then joined him in combat on Herb's third mission, going on to fly a total of 17 missions together. For reasons I haven't discovered, Sam Gardner changed crews for the 384th's Mission Number 73, and never flew on the Allison/Small crew again. It was by far the crew with whom he flew the most missions, his highest next total being only nine missions with other crews. His last mission was on April 19, 1944, and his End of Duty was

The Crew

April 26, 1944; one day before my Uncle Herb's plane went down over France. Gardner survived the war, was never a POW and came home to live a long life with his family.

Bombardier **2nd Lt. Jack C. Nagel** was a big man — six foot three — and a native of Houston, Texas, with the nickname "Big Foot." He enlisted in December of 1941, earlier than a lot of men, while he was still enrolled at Texas A & M University. At A & M, Nagel was a "Yell Leader," which is a group of five students that are elected annually by the student body to lead fans in a series of "Yells" during athletic events.

It's very likely that his enlistment into the military was in response to the attack on Pearl Harbor on December 7, 1941, as so many patriotic young men were inspired to enlist after that infamous day. He spent about a year working with the Army Corps of Engineers before transferring to the Army Air Force, where he would train to eventually become a bombardier with the 384th Bombardment Group. He flew a total of twenty-four missions with my Uncle Herb. His final, fatal mission was on May 8, 1944...which was tragically also his 24th birthday.

Tech Sgt. William F. Laubenstein — Radio Operator and Gunner Bill Laubenstein was just a regular guy from a small town in Upstate New York called Little Falls, and one of six kids. He went to school, worked jobs caddying at golf courses and as a counselor at summer camps in the Upstate area, and spent time in college at both Cornell and Purdue. At the age of 23, he wanted to volunteer for the service, so he enlisted in the Army Air Force because he wanted to learn to be a fighter pilot. Unfortunately, he had problems with his vision — his depth perception, specifically — which precluded him from being able to go into pilot training, so instead they sent him to machine gunnery training to learn on the .50-caliber that would be the main defensive weapon of the B-17.

T/Sgt. Laubenstein's story is pretty incredible, and I found it when researching what became of him after the war when I was able to contact some of family. He was a little older than most of the guys, at

Bombs Away

T/Sgt. William F. Laubenstein. (Photo courtesy of Laubenstein family.)

twenty-six years old when the crew formed up in 1943. He flew twenty-two missions with my uncle and was shot down with most of Herb Small's "regular" crew on May 8, 1944. He survived that crash, along with four other crew members, but was taken prisoner by the Germans after being betrayed by French Nazi sympathizers and collaborators who reported his presence to the enemy.

He was also part of a group I call "The Bills," though it has no basis in any historical reality, meaning I haven't seen them referred to in that way in any of the text or correspondence. There was, for a time, three different guys named "William" on the crew; there was T/Sgt. William F. Laubenstein, S/Sgt. William A. Clements (Engineer and Top Gunner), and for seven missions sprinkled throughout their overall mission record, there was S/Sgt. William L. Kouski, (Waist/Flex Gunner). I

The Crew

like to think that the guys maybe had some fun with it, giving them funny nicknames, such as "Bill," "Billy," and "Willy," or maybe "Wild Bill" or something similar. Maybe "#1, #2 and #3?" Probably not...but maybe.

In his official record of his wartime experience...his memoirs really, self-published mainly for his family and friends, loaned to me by his niece...he talks very affectionately about meeting the love of his life, Josephine ("Pep") Miklave (also from Little Falls), and marrying her while he was in training.

So many of these men did not come home to reunite with their sweethearts. Thankfully, William Laubenstein did. He survived the war and went home to start a family that still thrives today. There is more on his experience as a POW later. He was awarded the Purple Heart for wounds received in battle. However, he didn't actually receive the medal until 2008 — sixty-four years later! During an interview for the belated award ceremony in a local Colorado newspaper, he told the reporter, "The reason I never stopped to get it is after I was discharged I wanted

Tremblin Gremlin fueling up. (Courtesy of 384thBombGroup.com).

The Natural

to get home." He was more interested in getting home to his wife and family than he was in receiving a medal, which says a lot about the kind of man he was; family meant more to him than accolades. It was because of the determined efforts of his family — his niece, and her husband, in particular, that he finally received the medal he was awarded in 1944. Bill's niece, Erin Dowd, retired US Army Colonel and her husband Jake Thompson, a retired Army Green Beret MSG and Company SGM, advocated for the medal Bill earned in 1944.

Erin shared with me the personal story: "Bill rarely spoke of his combat service. He and Jake established rapport, discussed combat experiences, and through their conversations over a year, Jake realized that Uncle Bill was not in receipt of VA care. Further, Jake discovered that Uncle Bill was injured in combat but never spoke of a Purple Heart. Jake immediately coordinated with his congressman, provided the required evidence, and tenaciously ensured the Purple Heart was awarded in 2008. Together Erin and Jake worked with the US Air Force Academy in Colorado Springs to ensure Uncle Bill's Purple Heart was ceremoniously recognized by a General Officer."

He described the relationship between the officers and the enlisted men in his war memoirs as follows: "The officers were down to earth people and respected us. The pilots elevated us in rank, and I became a Staff Sargeant and after 10 missions became a Tech Sargeant. This meant a pay raise, which was great. We were flying every day and getting good ratings."

There isn't much to be found regarding **Tech Sergeant William A. Clements**, the crew's Engineer and Top Turret gunner, and the second of my imagined group of "The Bills." He was from Cincinnati, Ohio and was laid to rest in nearby Milford, Ohio after he was Killed in Action in 1944 and brought home. He was one of the original Earl Allison crew and flew on twenty-three missions with Herb Small. Though they were not flying together on their respective final missions, the outcomes were the same.

The Crew

The eyes of the plane at the "six o'clock" position for most of their missions were those of Tail Gunner **Staff Sergeant Kenneth N. Hougard**, who flew twenty-one of his twenty-seven total credited missions with Herbert Small. On at least two occasions, when the ranking officers Capt. James Merritt and Col. Dale O. Smith subbed in as pilot, Herb moved to the back of the plane to man the tail gun and Sgt. Hougard moved to the Waist Gunner position. According to the memoirs of Col. Dale O. Smith, titled *Screaming Eagle - Memoirs of a B-17 Group Commander*, this unusual positioning of a pilot in the tail gunner spot was a policy that he specifically enacted with the 384th because of his strong belief in flying a very tight formation. "I had required an experienced pilot to ride in the tail gunner's position on lead airplanes and report any poor formation flying." Col. Smith was a stickler for tight formation flying as a defensive measure against enemy fighters, and he believed that the 384th, under his command, was the only Bomb Group to employ such a policy.

Sgt. Hougard's story is one of the most captivating of the entire crew, as he featured in a very harrowing Evade and Escape tale that is

Kenneth Hougard was the artist (and maybe the humorist) of the group. (Picture courtesy of Laubenstein Family.)

retold in his exact words later in this book. In brief, when the B-17 carrying him and the rest of Earl Allison's crew, minus Herb Small, was shot down on May 8th over the Sottevast area of Normandy, France, Sgt. Hougard was able to parachute from the doomed Fortress and land successfully in German occupied France. With help from French citizens and the French Underground Resistance, and using his own cunning and wits, he was able to evade capture, first by hiding in various barns and farms, then later by being actively helped and hidden by the French Resistance. He was eventually rescued, very fittingly, on July 4th, 1944 — his own Independence Day of a sort — by the invading American and Allied forces in Normandy, nearly four weeks after D-Day.

After the war, he returned home to Portland, Oregon to his wife Adelaide Virginia Hawks and raised two children. He became an insurance agent, possibly a fitting career for a man all too familiar with the concept of risk. He eventually moved to Las Vegas, Nevada and spent his final thirteen years there, passing away in March of 2012 at the age of 89. Hopefully in Las Vegas he was finally able to shake the chill of the Grafton-Underwood winter and 25,000-foot missions from his bones.

The most frequent hands on a waist gun for the Allison/Small crew were those of native Chicagoan **Staff Sergeant James H. Grimmett**. He was at his post amidship for twenty-one of Herb's missions; and received Combat Mission Credit for twenty-four missions in all. Knowing that soldiers, sailors and airmen were often very superstitious, one has to wonder if dire thoughts were going through Sgt. Grimmett's mind on the morning of May 8th, as the crew took off without Herb Small, whose Fort had been gunned down only a week and a half earlier. I know from the words of 1st Lt. Joseph Cittadini in his self-published war memoirs *20th Mission: A short account as well as my memory serves*, that the men felt the loss of Herb Small and their other lost comrades in their daily routine. Cittadini made specific mention of it; "Fioretti, Bailey, Merlo, Griffiths, Small, Brookings, Big T and many more fine young men are gone now. As I think of them, I say a little prayer for them and their families. I'm feeling low and my mind is still clouded because of

The Crew

insufficient sleep."

Grimmett was one of the four survivors of the Allison crew who bailed out of *Reno's Raider* on the May 8th mission on their supposed "Milk Run" over the Normandy region of France. He made it safely to the ground, which in itself is a small miracle, with the enemy firing at him on the way down. Then, after briefly hiding out with some French citizens, he was betrayed by French collaborators and turned over to the Germans, and spent the remainder of the war as a Prisoner of War in Stalag Luft IV, coincidentally with his pal William Laubenstein.

James Grimmett was awarded the Air Medal with three Oak Leaf clusters for his service. After the war, he married his sweetheart Adeline, lived a long life and passed away on August 1st of 1997, at the age of 77.

Pivoting to the belly of the plane, we would find **Staff Sgt. Vernon L. Kaufman** of Haddam, Kansas manning the Ball Turret for twenty-four of Herb Small's missions. The Ball Turret position was as dangerous and lonely a spot as there was on the B-17; once the gunner was in position, he had to stay there in the cramped and restricted space, often suffering muscle cramps, claustrophobia and debilitating cold. If he had to relieve himself while in the ball turret, he had only one very uncomfortable option, which was to just let it go. Many ball turret gunners fashioned special improvised gadgets and devices to help with this issue, because if they didn't, the inevitable result was that the unfortunate liquid would freeze in their clothing and even on the glass of the turret, making things worse in two ways.

Vernon Kaufman kept a very interesting, handwritten journal of his missions, which was given, along with the rest of his personal effects, to his family after the war. His sister, Donna (Kaufman) Wiley — age ninety as of 2024 — still has that journal to this day and was gracious enough to share a copy of it with me. The journal gives us a small glimpse of the war through her brother's eyes, just twenty-two years old at the time, seeing the war from his perch beneath a B-17 Flying Fortress. He offered technical details on many of the missions, such as the amount of flak or types of enemy fighters that were encountered, along with more casual observations on the weather and places of interest they flew over during missions.

[One thing I have had to often remind myself of while working on this story is remember that these men, however mature or tough they may have been, were still very young men. I have to remind myself of his youth in particular when I read Vernon Kaufman's journal; these are the observations of someone barely out of his teens. How grand the skies over Europe must have seemed — flying over some of the most famous cities of history and literature — to someone of humble beginnings who maybe hadn't ventured very far out of Kansas before joining the Army Air Force.]

He wrote few words, but they seemed to say a lot. His remarks on their mission of December 24, 1943, merely stated, "No flak or fighters. Easy run. Hougard is in the hospital at Leicester. Our altitude was 12,000 feet." On a later mission over Schweinfurt, he noted that "The vicinity of Schweinfurt looks like the Black Hills of South Dakota."

Vernon Kaufman was awarded a Gold Star, Purple Heart, the American Campaign Medal, the Army Presidential Unit Citation, the Air Medal with three Oak Leaf Clusters and the Distinguished Flying Cross for his service and sacrifice in World War II, making him one of the most decorated men of the crew.

Rounding out the Allison Crew are the last two men who flew with them the most…including the last of my "Three Bills" cohort — **Staff Sergeant William L. Kouski** — and **1st Lieutenant Joseph L. G. Cittadini**. These two men were on eight and five missions respectively with my uncle Herb and met very different fates in the end. Flex/Waist Gunner S/Sgt. Kouski was, for reasons I have not discovered, busted down to Private and transferred out of the 384th to the Military Police in orders dated May 10, 1944, and was therefore not on either of the fatal

The Crew

missions. He survived the war and was eventually discharged from duty on September 5, 1944. He was awarded the Air Medal and went home to marry June A. (Avery) Kouski. He died on September 24, 2006, at the age of eighty-three, and is buried in the Cordova Cemetery in Rock Island County, Illinois.

Navigator Lt. Cittadini, another of the "Old Men" of the crew at age twenty-seven, was born in Montreal, Canada, and at the age of eleven, his family moved to Brooklyn, New York, which must have been a major culture shock for the young man. He joined the Army Air Force on August 14, 1943 at twenty-seven years of age, surrounded by younger men who probably shaved once a week, whether they needed to or not. These older men were often teased and nicknamed "Gramps," but were in fact highly respected and seen as a source of life experience and wisdom to the much younger men. It's hard to imagine someone considering a twenty-seven-year-old man "old," but that's how it was for these guys.

Despite not being on the ill-fated missions of April 27th or May 8th with Herb Small or Earl Allison, where many of his most-frequent crew members were lost, Cittadini also ran out of luck in the end. In his case, he was flying in the B-17 *Goin' Dog* for his 20th mission on May 7th, just one day before the Allison crew, minus the previously lost Herb Small, went down on May 8th. It seems that in those tense days of March, April and May 1944, there was almost no escaping fate for many of the 384th, and indeed the entire 8th Air Force.

Lt. Cittadini's plane experienced, according to the Sortie Report, engine difficulties that forced it to turn back from the mission while they were over enemy territory, after which they had to jettison their bombs and crash land near Jade, Germany. The whole crew survived the crash and spent the remainder of the war as a POWs, primarily at Stalag Luft III in Sagen-Silesia in Bavaria. Later they were moved to Stalag 13-D in Nuremberg-Langwasser, also in Bavaria. He survived the war and was sent back to Florida and eventually Texas to rehab his injuries, for which he received the Purple Heart after the war. He remained a reserve officer until 1968, and spent his last years in Melbourne, Florida. He passed

Bombs Away

away at age ninety-three, on December 22, 2009, with the rank of Lt. Colonel.

The last crew my uncle ever flew with was all guys he had never flown with before. It was also his very first mission as pilot, rather than co-pilot or tail gunner. This was the crew of the April 27, 1944 mission over France:

- 2nd Lt. Herbert W. Small — Pilot
- 2nd Lt. Roy J. Morris — Co-Pilot
- 2nd Lt. James E. McGue — Navigator
- 2nd Lt. John M. Sewack — Bombardier
- St. Sgt. Marion L. Parker — Radio Operator
- Sgt. Richard D. Pirrello — Engineer/Top Turret
- Sgt. John B. Reynolds — Ball Turret Gunner
- Sgt. Edward J. Potkay — Tail Gunner
- St. Sgt. David E. George — Waist (Flex) Gunner
- Sgt. Russell H. Ulrich — Waist (Flex) Gunner

A waist gunner poses for a photo at his gun.
(Courtesy of Paul Teal and Sam Coleman.)

The Crew

The rest of the men — of the forty-eight in total — with whom my great-uncle flew are listed here. They each flew fewer than five missions with him; many of them only one mission, but they are all part of his story, and the story of the 384th. Thus far, twenty-seven of the men who flew with Herb have been mentioned in this narrative, leaving twenty-one more who flew at least one mission with Herbert Small. None are trivial. None should be forgotten. These are those men.

- 2nd Lt. David L. McKinney — Navigator
- Tech. Sgt. Doy J. Cloud — Radio Operator
- St. Sgt. Roy F. Howell — Waist (Flex) Gunner
- Tech. Sgt. Deston K. Cleland — Tail Gunner
- St. Sgt. Alfred A. Clark — Tail Gunner
- St. Sgt. Lawrence M. Hall — Tail Gunner
- St. Sgt. John Narog — Waist (Flex) Gunner
- St. Sgt. William L. Harper — Waist (Flex) Gunner
- St. Sgt. John J. Stevens — Waist (Flex) Gunner
- St. Sgt. Angelo A. LaSalle — Waist (Flex) Gunner

- 2nd Lt. John J. Fallon — Navigator
- St. Sgt. Leland R. Smith — Waist (Flex) Gunner
- St. Sgt. James J. Fisher — Tail Gunner
- St. Sgt. George Ursta — Ball Turret Gunner
- Tech. Sgt. William W. Hutchison — Top Turret
- Tech. Sgt. Ernest L. Frazier — Radio Operator
- Tech. Sgt. Alan B. Purdy — Radio Operator
- Capt. James M. Merritt — Pilot/Co-Pilot
- Col. Dale O. Smith — Pilot/Co-Pilot
- Capt. Arthur J. Drogue — Navigator
- St. Sgt. David E. George — Waist (Flex) Gunner

*****

These were the men that my uncle Herb flew with during his

Bombs Away

missions over Europe in World War II. Some were barely out of high school. Some were "aged veterans" at twenty-six or twenty-eight years old. They ranked everywhere from Private to Colonel. They came from cities and towns all over the country, like Haddam, Kansas; Rochester and Little Falls, New York; Cincinnati, Ohio; Omaha, Nebraska; Portland, Oregon; Chicago, Illinois; San Diego and Highlands, California; Reading, Pennsylvania; New London, Connecticut; Michigan and Colorado. And they also came from Sheffield and Beverly, Massachusetts. They came from all over the country with incredibly diverse backgrounds, upbringings, beliefs and life history…the kind of diversity that really matters…and joined with one another as a unit to face a common enemy that was threatening our freedom and our way of life. These men mattered then, and they matter now, which is part of the reason I tell this story, say their names and share with you what I can about each of them.

Alfred Nuttall with *Boomerang*. *(Courtesy of 384thBombGroup.com.)*

1943 Missions

6

Our big plane gracefully left the runway and climbed to see the rising sun over the dip of the horizon. The ground below was still in darkness as we joined the squadron formation. The time it takes to form the group was usually about six to ten minutes if all goes well. The sun was warm and pleasant and having set up my navigation aids and having a few minutes with nothing of importance to do I relaxed and dozed off. The intercom chatter quickly terminated my snooze.
- Lt. Col. Joseph Cittadini

Upon his arrival at Grafton-Underwood with his crew in late October 1943, Herb was greeted by weather in eastern England that was cold, wet and windy a good deal of the time, with average temperatures between 41- and 51-degrees Fahrenheit. Men were typically given a couple of weeks to get themselves used to the routine and trained on how the base and flight operations/missions generally worked. On his first mission, Herb flew with Captain Randolph Jacobs, who, as pre-

Bombs Away

Randolph Jacob's usual crew: L-R: Doy Cloud (Radio), Robert Compton (TG), Lawrence Wager (WG), Eugene Boger (CP), Randolph Jacobs (P), John Curtin (N), James Seibel (B), Donald Gorham (BT), Jack Goetz (E/TT), Aldo Gregori (Asst. Eng.). (Courtesy of 384thBombGroup.com)

viously mentioned, already had nine completed bombing missions on his resume, having begun his missions back in August of the same year. Capt. Jacobs was destined to cross ill-fated paths again with Herb when he took Herb's vacated spot on the Earl Allison crew roughly six months later. Randolph, with only three months of combat action to his credit was already considered a "seasoned veteran" at that point, and the new guys coming in looked up to him for it.

In *One Last Look*, Philip Kaplan and Rex Alan Smith describe further the crash-landing incident involving Jacobs in *El Rauncho*. The story about his return from an August 1943 mission to Schweinfurt seems to encapsulate the kind of pilot and the kind of man Randolph "Randy" "Moose" Jacobs was. Part of this story was related in the previous chapter…here is the rest: "Several of the landing aircraft came in firing double red flares, which signaled the waiting ambulances that

1943 Missions

wounded men were aboard. Some of the ships that had suffered little apparent damage carried dead men, while others that were so battered they appeared incapable of flying brought home crews not even scratched. One of those was the 384th's *El Rauncho* piloted by Randolph Jacobs. There were holes in its tail and both wings, its landing gear was unusable, and on final approach for a belly landing, two of its engines suddenly quit. Even so, Jacobs managed to put it on the runway where after a long spark-showered metal-shrieking slide, it finally came to rest, and its ten-man crew climbed out unhurt. Thereupon, Jacobs lit a cigar, looked at the remains of his airplane, and observed, 'Guess they just didn't want us to bomb their ol' nuts and bolts factory.'"

Herb arrived at the 384th during a very difficult time. Losses had been mounting, in large part due to the very limited range of the fighter escorts available at the time, which were mainly the P-47 Thunderbolt and the P-38 Lightning. Both were high quality fighters but lacked the fuel capacity and range to cover the entirety of some of the longer missions of the bombers. The Eighth Air Force desperately needed a fighter with longer range capabilities. Thankfully, they would soon have one.

October 14th, dubbed Black Thursday, was perhaps the low point for the Eighth Air Force, with yet another mission to Schweinfurt, Germany to bomb a ball-bearing factory taking a particularly heavy toll. It is described well here by Martin W. Bowman in *Castles in the Air*: "Sixty Fortresses and 600 men were missing. Five B-17s had crashed in England as a result of their battle-damaged conditions and twelve more were destroyed in crash landings or so badly damaged that they had to be written off." Nine aircraft from the 384th were lost on that day, erasing some ninety men from the lives at Grafton-Underwood and leaving a gaping hole in the roster and hearts of the base. Men who were newly arrived at the base were faced with the awkward and morbid task of moving their own gear into the quarters and bunks of those who had been recently lost, sometimes in barracks that were almost entirely empty. The last remaining (ie. surviving) residents were confronted with stark reminders of their lost pals by the presence of the fresh faces. This

Bombs Away

certainly had to lead to some tense moments between the men.

There is some opinion given on the reasons for the heavy losses of 1943 by Richard Overy in his work, *The Bombers and the Bombed*, with him referencing a file from the Air Force Historical Research Agency (AFHRA) from *Eighth Air Force Tactical Development 1942-1945* by McFarland and Newton: "The explanation for the slow evaluation of a long-range fighter capability lies not with the technology but with the Eighth Air Force Commanders. [Col. Ira] Eaker had always believed in the self-defending capability of the large daylight bomber formation. The prevailing tactical assumption in operations was 'the security of the force'; the larger the bomber stream, the more secure it would be." In short, the commanders, in their arrogance, thought that these great machines of war — the Flying Fortresses and Liberators — were capable of mounting all the defense necessary to prevail in battle against an incredibly skilled, innovative and capable enemy in the Luftwaffe. They believed this despite the hard fact of ever-mounting losses of men and aircraft. As often occurs with those detached from the leading edge of an issue, the theoretical trumped the practical.

[In my opinion, the arrogance and ignorance of the higher command are something that I believe cost many lives in the Eighth Air Force. Men who had possibly not even been in the air in a bomber in actual combat were making decisions based on assumptions made from hypotheticals in a officers' planning room somewhere, based not on the reality of battle in the air but on theory and speculation. The airmen seem to have been considered easily expendable assets to the higher command, to be hurled at the enemy in ever greater numbers because there were always more replacements on the way. Even if they had simply thought of the airmen coldly and logically as valuable assets on which they had spent a lot of the time and money, it may have made a difference. Even a

1943 Missions

cold, logical *financial* decision to change tactics and offer more protection could have meant fewer lives lost in the end.]

Another policy that both frustrated and infuriated many of the men in the bombers was the strict rule that no other crews were allowed to come to the aid of a B-17 (or B-24) in the event that it was damaged and forced out of formation, usually because it couldn't maintain speed or altitude. Once a plane was crippled by flak or German fighters and was separated from the Group, it became an easy target for the Luftwaffe and their fighters pounced like hyenas on a wounded gazelle. Many a crew had to watch helplessly as their friends and comrades were set upon by German fighters with only their own guns to defend themselves. Crews also knew that the shoe could very easily be on the other foot someday, when they would be the wounded Fort forced out of formation and left to their own fate.

Whether this was a wise tactical or strategic decision or not can be debated. I believe it was certainly a very cold and inhumane one that had to be yet another heavy blow to unit morale.

Command of the base, which had been under Col. Budd J. Peaslee since May 29, 1943, was transferred to interim Commander Col. Julius K. "Con" Lacey on September 6th, who then oversaw the horrific losses of October 1943 and Black Thursday, in particular. I don't doubt that he was indeed relieved when he finally *was relieved* of temporary command on November 24th. He passed the torch to the towering six-foot-six figure of Col. Dale O. Smith, who was then faced with the daunting task of turning around what he called in his memoirs the "poor performance record and low morale" of the 384th. He was charged with the task of getting the show back on the road, which seems fitting, since the 384th Bomber Group's motto was **"Keep the Show on the Road."**

The men were given a short respite in early November, after the disastrous month of October, because of inclement weather. According to *Castles in the Air*, by Martin W. Bowman, "For the first two weeks of

Bombs Away

Col. Dale O. Smith takes over command of Grafton-Underwood in October 1943. The towering Smith is shown with Col. Julius K. Lacey.
(Courtesy of 384thBombGroup.com)

November 1943, England was blanketed by thick, woolly fog and airfields were lashed with intermittent showers and high winds. However, on the morning of November 16, the bad weather lifted…and a mission to Norway went ahead as scheduled."

November 16th was the first mission for Herbert Small, and Randy Jacobs was in the pilot's seat to show him the ropes. Herb would not be with his regular crew until his third mission on December 13th, but that was standard for newly arrived pilots to get some time with a seasoned crew. The target for the November 16th mission was the Knaben II Molybdenum Mine, an industrial target in Knaben, Norway. Molybdenum is an element that is used to form ultra-hard, very stable steel alloys, with the sixth-highest melting point of any element. It was used in all sorts of weapons of war, from tanks to artillery cannons and beyond, and was vital to the German war effort in World War II.

According to R.J. Overy in *The Bombers and the Bombed*, "The typical instructions for a Bomber Command raid illustrate the close attention to planning detail and the range of demands made of the crews. Aircraft from four or five bomber groups were given instructions about force size, composition of the bomb load, routes to the destination target (or for the decoy attacks), and the timing of each of five waves of attacking aircraft, which had to drop their bombs within a twenty-minute period to maximize impact…The whole combat force typically extended for twenty miles, was six miles wide, and flew in staggered formation, the highest aircraft some 4,000 feet above the lowest."

Missions typically got started the evening before, when the orders were received at the base. Group Navigators and other planners would get to work coming up with the routes the planes would fly and other logistics vital to accomplishing the mission. Bomber crews would often wait anxiously around the base bulletin board to see which crews would be flying the next day's mission. The following morning, those flying would be woken up at around 3:30 a.m. by the "night owl," who was the unfortunate soul assigned the thankless task of getting the often exhausted and occasionally hungover men out of bed and pointing them in the direction of the mess hall for breakfast. That unpopular man was officially known as the Charge of Watch.

Radio Operator Tech Sgt. William Laubenstein gave a good summary of the usual preparation for bombing missions in his book, *A Quiet Hero*;

"Preparations for bomb missions:
- Usually notified 7:30 or 8:00 PM the night before
- Breakfast at 4:30 AM
- Briefing at 5:00 AM with pins and thread on a corkboard.
- Rundown of the weather, flak and fighter protection.
- Take-off time 6:30 AM - 1 plane every 15 seconds.
- Briefing ends with a time tick as all watches are synchronized."

Bombs Away

2nd Lt. Joseph L.G. Cittadini, navigator on five missions with Herb Small, described the morning of a particular mission in 1944. You can almost feel through his words the exhaustion he was battling; "My mind is dull and my body is tired. I shake my head in a vane effort to release the tension of my neck muscles. I try massaging the back of my neck but that too offers no relief. Two and a half hours sleep after a week of carousing in Scotland on flak leave is hardly enough for me. I am fatigued, mentally and physically. Ted and Jeff, [Ted Goller and 2nd Lt. James Jefferson Brown] my roommates and good buddies, are getting ready, too. We have nothing to say to each other. We are automatons responding as robots do, without conscious thought. We were all too tired and uninspired to think, let alone talk.

"When I'm ready, I gather up my briefcase of navigation equipment, sling my knapsack containing my escape articles over my shoulder and hurry out into the cold darkness. With flashlight in hand as a headlight for my bike, I pedal wearily off to the base mess hall about a mile away."

These are some of the items that the escape kits contained:

- Horlicks tablets - (candy for energy)
- Chocolate
- Milk (tube)
- Benzadrine tablets (fatigue)
- Halazone tablets (water purifier)
- Matches
- Adhesive tape
- Chewing gum
- Water bottle
- Compass
- Maps
- File (hacksaw)
- Foreign currency

1943 Missions

Breakfast for the men flying each day's mission would include fresh eggs, as opposed to the usual (and highly unpopular) powdered eggs, along with coffee, toast and other usual breakfast fare. Cittadini described the powdered eggs as "...an abomination invented by some guy back in the States who, it seems, was doing his share to help Germany win the war."

The mission briefing would commence around 4:30, although those flying in the lead positions, plus pilots, navigators and bombardiers, would have additional meetings with additional details on the route and the target. The men would file into the briefing room, already starting to fill with a haze of cigarette smoke, and await the eventual "At-ten-tion!" when a senior officer would enter the room and begin the briefing. In the front of the room would be a large curtain covering a map of Northern Europe, with the bombing route, so carefully planned by the Group Navigator, designated by colored string tacked to it, with the target highlighted, as well.

Crews would receive information about expected fighter resistance, flak (German anti-aircraft fire), altitude, cloud cover and weather conditions. At Grafton-Underwood, the 384th's weather man was nicknamed "Cloudy," which was not an unusual nickname for the men in that role throughout the bases in the UK. Another popular moniker was "Stormy." Sometimes there were cheers for a high-profile target or a "milk run" — a mission that was expected to be easy with little enemy resistance — and other times there were groans for targets that were expected to be long, difficult and more dangerous.

Allan Healey, retired from the Royal Air Force, had a very poignant comment about briefings: "By map, picture and diagram, the whole operation was explained. [The Intelligence Officer] put on the route, target...expected flak and fighters...[and] weather: an operation of death told like a commuter's timetable."

After the briefing, the men would go through the arduous process of putting on all of their gear, including flak suits and cold weather gear, plus escape kits, and finally carry it all, plus a few large .50-cal machine guns, to the trucks waiting to bring them to their planes. William

Bombs Away

Laubenstein was able to provide some detail about how the men outfitted themselves to survive the exceedingly cold temperatures on missions:

"• Temperatures can be severely cold, especially over the North Sea, it can drop to 60 degrees F below zero.
• Fleece lined leather pants and a sheep-skin bomber jacket.
• A Mae West life jacket, parachute and oxygen mask.
• Sometimes a flak jacket."

While all this was going on, tirelessly working ground crews were busy putting the finishing touches on repairs, fueling, ammunition and bombloads, making sure every single plane on the mission was ready to fly and fight at its best. The ground crews were often the unsung heroes of the base, working day and night on all manner of repairs and replacements, bringing sometimes heavily damaged Forts back to life. They poured their blood, sweat and tears into their ships to get them ready to

A Group of B-17s in formation. (Courtesy of 384thBombGroup.com)

fly for the men that were putting themselves in the thick of the fight, and they endured the cold and wet English weather in the process, often for hours in the dead of night.

Once they were in their Flying Fortresses, the men would go through their thorough preflight checklist to make sure each system was working properly, and all of the switches were toggled to the right positions. Seventeen different items had to be checked off as 'ready to go,' such as Fuel Transfer Valves, Cowl Flaps, Turbos, De-icers, Throttles and Generators. There was another sequence for starting the engines, another for engine "run-up" and then two more sets of items for before and after take-off. And finally, there was a checklist, circumstances permitting, at the end of the mission for landing and on final approach. Nothing that the crews were able to control was left to chance.

After take-off, which was often a miraculous feat in and of itself, because the planes were loaded with so much gear, fuel and ammunition they were often well over their supposed maximum weight, the process of "forming up" came next. Sometimes it took as much as an hour to get all the planes into the proper formation. Cloud cover, fog and rain made this especially challenging, with mid-air collisions being all too real and frequent. Sadly, about five percent of the Eighth Air Force aircraft lost in World War II were the result of accidents during the process of forming up at the very beginning of missions.

For Herb's first mission — aboard a B-17 with no name — to the Knaben II Molybdenum mine on November 16th, the 384th Bomber Group led the 41st Combat Wing and 1st Bomb Division. They were heading some 525 miles northeast of Grafton-Underwood to southern Norway, over the often ill-tempered North Sea…not a place a bomber crew wanted to ditch if they experienced trouble. Survival time for crews who ditched in the frigid North Sea was often measured in minutes rather than hours. The weather report described moderate cloud cover, strong turbulence and good visibility en-route to Norway over the North Sea. (Cloud cover was reported on a "tenths" fractional scale, with five-tenths being fifty percent coverage and so on.) They were ex-

Bombs Away

pected to reach the target around 1230 - 1300 hours, which would be two and a half to three hours of flight time one-way once they assembled and left England.

Once they were over the ocean, the crews would test their guns, with each gunner firing a few rounds to make sure each one was working properly. When enemy fighters were rapidly closing in, it was no time to find out that a gun was jammed or otherwise malfunctioning. Upon reaching 10,000 feet of altitude, the pilot, who was the absolute leader on the B-17, would alert the men to don their masks to begin breathing from the ship's oxygen system. The higher up they went, the thinner the air got and the colder the temperature became, with temps at 20,000 feet around thirty-five degrees below zero, and at 26,000 feet a stunning fifty-three degrees below zero. Touching any of the plane's metal with bare hands would mean their skin would freeze tight to it, causing serious

Flak on a 384th Bomb Group Mission. Notice the "P" insignia on the tail of the Forts. (Courtesy of 384thBombGroup.com)

1943 Missions

injuries. The men also had to be careful with the oxygen masks at the higher, colder altitudes, because condensation from their breath could freeze inside their masks or the supply tubes and restrict or cut off the flow of oxygen. If they weren't paying attention, they could suddenly pass out, and in the case of the tail or ball gunners, it might go unnoticed. Many crews had a policy of doing a quick verbal check-in over the intercom every ten or fifteen minutes whenever they were on the oxygen system, especially at high altitudes.

A total of twenty-one Forts were assigned to this mission, assembled in three groups of seven, with a Lead Group, Low Group and High Group forming the Combat Box to be able to provide as much protection to each individual plane by way of the high number of guns they could bring to bear as a unit. One plane had to abort after take-off due to a loose oil line on an engine, so twenty planes remained to attack the Molybdenum mine. Flak was reported as "trailing and inaccurate" or "away and behind," and not much of a threat once they were over enemy territory. The lead plane reported no visibility on crossing the Norwegian Coast, such that they accidentally overflew the target area, prompting them to turn around and re-orient for another run. On the second pass, they were able to identify enough features along the route and pick up their target, which allowed them to begin the bombing run. However, at the bomb release point, the bombs in the lead plane would not release, so they were forced to make yet another pass over the target, only to find that the bombs still would not release. They radioed the Deputy Leader and said they "would make the complete run and would give him the signal by a red lamp when to release his bombs."

Randy Jacobs, following the signal from the Group Leader, dropped his twelve 500-pound bombs from 13,600 feet on the Knaben II Molybdenum mine, with results described simply as "Good" in the sortie report. Other planes in the group reported bombs that missed the target or even failed to drop from the plane, so the overall results were quite varied. The secondary target for the mission, should the first not be visible, was Oslo, but it was not needed for this mission because most

Bombs Away

of the planes were able to drop on or near the primary target.

The Molybdenum mine target was reported in the mission records as "one of the smallest and most concentrated [targets] ever attacked by the Eight Air Force, and because of its size and the natural and artificial camouflage, it presented a problem in expert navigation and called for exactness in precision bombing." The difficulty was described in the Sortie Report: "We dropped down to 14,000 feet to bomb and did not drop any lower because the Low Group would be in the clouds. We could not find the target. None of the other groups seemed to be able to find it either, so we went back out to the coastline to orient ourselves. We came back in, and thought we were on target, but we were not sure, so we did not drop our bombs. We made three more bomb runs trying to release our bombs, but they would not release...", which led to the lead pilot having to signal the other planes when it was time to drop their

Radio man Tech. Sgt. Doy J. Cloud, (Courtesy of 384thBombGroup.com)

1943 Missions

"Bombs Away!" from an unnamed B-17G in the 384th.
(Courtesy of 384thBombGroup.com

bombs.

After "bombs away," it was time to get out of Dodge and head back home as quickly and directly as possible, since enemy fighters and flak were still doing their best to knock the Forts out of the sky. All twenty ships made it home, but the Jacobs crew, with Herb Small in the co-pilot's seat, was forced to land about 136 miles north of Grafton-Underwood at RAF Lissett, due to a fuel shortage, possibly the result of the multiple runs at the target that were probably not factored into the fuel load. That sort of landing was much preferred to having to ditch in the North Sea or English Channel, where men could drown or freeze in the icy waters before rescuers could get to them.

Once the crews were safely back on the ground at base and the wounded had been removed (planes signaled to the ground crews with red flares if they had wounded aboard, and thus were given priority to land), the men headed to the post-mission 'interrogation,' where they would be debriefed on as much detail as they could remember about every aspect of the mission. They would be greeted by hot cups of coffee and double shots of whiskey from base personnel and WAAC or Red Cross volunteers. Every possible detail of the mission would be gleaned from each of the men for the records; number of enemy fighters; bombing results; flak types, accuracy and amounts; details on planes that were damaged or shot down; number of parachutes, if any, seen from doomed aircraft; routes; cloud cover; weather conditions; everything that could be remembered was recorded in great detail.

Roger Freeman, in *The Mighty Eighth War Manual,* remarked on the process. "As soon as crews had deposited their equipment and taken refreshment, they were called into the briefing room for interrogations. In their absence, the room had been rearranged so that sufficient chairs for a crew and an interrogating officer were placed around each table… Each interrogating officer was provided with a standard set of questions covering target observations, flak and fighter opposition, where encountered, tactics, fighter claims, weather, fighter support, aircraft in distress, plus other pertinent observations and suggestions."

[A big controversy at the time, and even to this day among historians and war history buffs, was the difference between the strategies employed for bombing by the Americans Eighth Air Force and the British Royal Air Force (RAF). The Americans chose to bomb during the daytime (known as "Precision High-Altitude Daytime Bombing), which was the far more accurate of the two methods, and spared the lives of untold numbers of civilians in both Germany and the occupied countries. Normally, the American bombers would not drop their bombs if they could not visually identify their primary or secondary targets, choosing instead to drop them in the Channel or North Sea on the way back to base. Unfortunately,

daytime bombing was also far more dangerous for the men flying those bombers, because it made them a much more susceptible target for enemy fighters and flak.

The British, on the other hand, preferred nighttime bombing, and made little effort to visually identify their targets, dropping their bombs only by navigational data. This led to highly inaccurate bombing and massive amounts of collateral damage and death, but a far lower casualty rate among their bomber crews. It also led to a much higher level of resentment by the German populace, in particular, such that British crews who were shot down often received much rougher treatment by German citizens and soldiers on the ground compared to the Americans.]

After his first mission, it was almost two weeks before Herb was back up in the air with the Randy Jacobs crew again, on the same plane without a name (AC# 237828). There were two new faces for him on this mission — Navigator 2nd. Lt. David W. McKinney and Radio Operator Tech. Sgt. Doy J. Cloud — and this time, they were headed for a port area in Bremen, Germany. A total of twenty-three aircraft from the 384th were scheduled to make this mission, but one scrubbed, six aborted and one failed to take off, leaving only fifteen Forts from the 384th to join the wing and make the run to Bremen. The 384th was the lead for the 41st Combat Wing, with the 303rd Bomber Group in the Low Group and the 379th Bomber Group in the High Group.

The lead plane for the 384th lost two superchargers on its engines, which slowed the whole formation down, so the other two Groups moved on ahead and left the 384th behind. It was reported that the flak was moderate, inaccurate and low over the target area, which had to have been a relief for everyone. Fighter escort, known to the bomber crews as "Our Little Friends," was very good, and it was reported that they had

Bombs Away

fighter coverage "from the time we hit the German coast." There were a high number of enemy fighters that were attacking from below the formation with rockets, so the "Little Friends" would have been especially welcome.

There was heavy cloud coverage from 6/10ths to 8/10ths, which meant the bombers had to use the relatively new PFF (Pathfinder Force) radar equipment installed on specially equipped B-17s of the 482nd Bomb Group, which allowed the planes to locate targets through thick clouds and overcast. The PFF planes would take the lead and then drop flares to signal when it was time for the formation to drop their bombs. One downside to this method of delivering their bombs was that they had no way to assess the damage to the target, or indeed even to know whether or not the target was actually hit. After "bombs away," it was time to head back home to England, and all of the 384th ships made it back safely, thanks in large part to the solid fighter escort they received nearly all the way back to base.

On December 13, 1943, after another two-week break, with two successful missions under his belt, it was time for Herb Small to rejoin his regular crew of Earl Allison, Sam Gardner and "the Bills," along with the rest of the guys. It had to feel good to get back with the team with whom he had trained and flown for so many months. I liken it to a football or baseball team who gets one of their key players back after an injury or some other hiatus; it's nice to get that missing piece back and get back in sync with each other. Anyone who has been part of a good team knows that there is a certain bond and camaraderie that develops, as well as almost a sixth sense about what your teammates are going to say or do at a particular time. It's part of what allows a team to elevate their game and become something greater than merely the sum of their parts.

The rest of the Allison crew had flown two missions in November, as well, with Lt. Eugene A. Boger riding shotgun with Earl in the cockpit in place of Herb. By November, Boger was already well seasoned himself, with nine successful missions and eight aborted missions, as the usual co-pilot with the Randy Jacobs crew. Likely both Boger and Herb

1943 Missions

Small were glad to get back with their "regular" guys for the next one.

Herb's third mission, on December 13th, had him and his regular crew heading back to battle in the B-17G *Little Barney*, the Fortress that they had ferried over from the States a few months earlier and one that would be a regular for them in the months to come. The target was once again the port area of Bremen, where there was known to be a Focke-Wulf-190 plant and submarine pens, both of which were crucial and deadly components of the German war machine. *Little Barney* was part of the Low Group in this raid, with the Lead Group also being supplied by the 384th, which had scheduled forty Forts for the mission. Six planes, including the Allison/Small crew on their first mission together, had to abort and return early.

For *Little Barney,* it was low oil pressure on engine #2 and another engine on fire that caused them to abort; both pretty good reasons to throw in the towel, as far as I'm concerned! They jettisoned their bombs in the North Sea (so they wouldn't risk landing with 6,000 pounds of explosives in the bomb bay) and headed back to England, "landing away" at Attlebridge, another base roughly seventy-five miles to the east of Grafton-Underwood. Thirty-four B-17s completed the mission, dropping their bombs, once again using the PFF radar system, because of heavy cloud cover over the target.

Ball Turret Gunner on the Allison/Small crew Vernon Kaufman described the aborted mission in his hand-written mission journal: "We were ready to fly over enemy territory when one of our motors ran away. Then we started back to England. On the road back we lost altitude very badly, so we [jettisoned] the bombs, threw the guns overboard and a lot of other stuff. We wrecked our plane *Little Barney* when we landed, somewhere on the north coast of England."

Lead plane for the Low Group was flown by Captain Alfred C. Nuttall and Captain James M. Merritt. Herb Small never flew with Captain Nuttall, but the two knew each other and crossed paths indirectly, by way of the B-17 named after the Captain, *Nuttall's Nut House*, in which Herb flew his last successful mission on April 9, 1944.

With the third mission aborted and not counting for "Combat

Bombs Away

Col. Alfred Nuttall in the cockpit. (Courtesy of 384thBombGroup.com)

Mission Credit" toward the mandatory twenty-five missions the men were required to fly to earn their way back home, the December 16th mission back to Bremen would check off number three for Earl Allison and his crew. This was the second of three raids on Bremen in December of 1943. The crews often became frustrated with the "Brass" (the high-ranking officers in charge) when they had to duplicate missions, which were often flown via the same routes as the previous missions with almost no variation, making it easier for the Germans to anticipate their routes and put up a stronger, more effective defense.

For this mission, now flying in *Sea Hag*, the Allison/Small crew was assigned to the role of "Flying Spare," which meant they would take off with the rest of the group and fly with them for the early part of the route, to be called on as a replacement if a ship was forced to drop out for any reason. Base Commander Col. Dale O. Smith was leading the group from the 384th with 2nd Lt. Edgar E. Ulrey aboard *Flak House*. Herb

1943 Missions

and the crew were tapped to replace another Fort with mechanical troubles, so *Sea Hag* fell in behind Smith's lead plane in the Low position for the run on Bremen to eliminate transportation targets. A total of twelve Fortresses were lost on that mission, fortunately none of them were from the 384th. All eighteen ships from the 384th that attempted the mission returned safely to England.

1943 was a year of sacrifice for the men. It was a year in which mission came first. Never was that more evident than when the next mission for the Allison/Small crew -- minus Tail Gunner Kenneth Hougard, who was in the hospital at Leicester, replaced by Sgt. Destin K. Cleland for the next two missions -- was scheduled for Christmas Eve. From Martin Bowman's *Castles in the Air*: "The Eighth was stood down on December 23rd, but missions resumed on Christmas Eve when the B-17s were dispatched to mysterious targets in France, which went under the codename 'Noball.'"

This mission would be Herb's first over Occupied France, and "Noball" was the codename for a V-1 Rocket launch sites, this one in particular in Croisette, France. The V-Weapons, or Vengeance Weapons, as some called them, were a final, futile effort by the Germans to tip the scales of war back in their favor as it became clear that they were going to lose. (More on those later.) It was one of the shortest missions the 384th would fly, at under 200 miles "as the crow flies," just over the coast of France and about 100 miles north of Paris. There had to be some grumbles amongst the crews for a Christmas Eve mission, but perhaps there was an angel flying alongside the Fortresses on that special day, because they reported no flak and no fighters, and all twenty-seven crews returned safely to base at Grafton-Underwood. None of them had to miss Christmas Day.

Christmas 1943 at Grafton-Underwood came with as much cheer and good will as men at war can muster. Men desperately missing their parents, wives, sweethearts, siblings and children had to make merry with each other and their surrogate families in Jolly Old England. Many of the men spent the day with those local families with whom they had become close…like real family…and the bases hosted their own reciprocal displays of holiday cheer and generosity. Again, from Bowman's *Castles in the Air:* "On Christmas Day the festivities got into full swing throughout the region. Americans dined with their English hosts, and deprived and orphaned children were invited to the bases for Christmas dinner and afternoon parties." Nothing warms the hearts of men like the smiles and laughter of children.

The end of 1943 brought about New Year's Eve, and with it came the year's final mission for the 384th. According to Col. Dale Smith's memoirs, the mission was originally not scheduled. "The last day of 1943 dawned with the usual thick overcast and a weeping sky. We had been promised a "stand-down" by Division, and I planned a New Year's celebration for all hands. They had been working awfully hard under my whip, but were making real progress and everyone certainly deserved a chance to cut loose. But our promised stand-down went up in smoke when we got a frag order to seek out and destroy a German blockade runner [ship] in the mouth of the Garonne River in southwestern France."

Unfortunately, there was 10/10 cloud cover for that target, and 8/10 for the secondary target, so the formation returned without attacking either. Many Forts jettisoned their bombs over the Channel, some returned to base fully loaded, with several others "landing away" at various other bases. One crew ditched and bailed out in the vicinity of Offham, Sussex (UK) and another crash-landed near Whittlesey, UK. It was not a very successful New Year's Eve bombing campaign, but bringing everyone back to England alive had to add to the evening's good cheer, and hopefully the supplies for Col. Smith's planned party didn't go to waste.

With three more missions completed in December, Herb Small's mission total was up to five; he was on his way towards the twenty-five mission goal. Upon the successful completion of their fifth mission, the men received an Air Medal, and for each additional five missions, a small Oak Leaf Cluster pin was awarded to be added to the Air Medal.

From R. J. Overy's *The Bombers and the Bombed*; "Somehow or

Ole Tulik

other all the detailed calculations, operating plans, and contingencies had to be mastered and put into effect by the expensively trained crews. There was always to be a gap between the ideal operation laid down by the military bureaucracy that ran the offensives and reality of combat..."
"Given the technical sophistication of much of the equipment, the large number of freshman crews to be initiated on each operation, and the vagaries of weather and navigation, it is perhaps surprising that bombing operations achieved as much as they did. Almost all the flight crews were between the ages of eighteen and twenty-five, a large number of them between eighteen and twenty-one; a few who lied about their age flew heavy bombers aged just seventeen. Almost nothing of what they experienced in training could prepare them for what happened by day or by night over Germany."

The first two and a half months of Herbert Small's war had gone relatively smoothly. His crew was meshing and working as a cohesive unit and they were having some very successful missions, contributing to the war effort for which they had trained for over a year back in the States. The close of the year must have been bittersweet for these men, having managed to survive, but also having seen many of their brothers in arms killed or missing in action. Replacement crews, like my Uncle Herb's, had by then earned the respect of the veteran crews and were now firmly a part of life at Grafton-Underwood.

But the hard work wasn't over yet. Although January started the year off a little slowly with only two missions, February would more than make up for it with ten missions stacked almost on top of each other. Things were about to get very intense for the 384th Bombardment Group and all of the Eighth Air Force.

Bombs Away

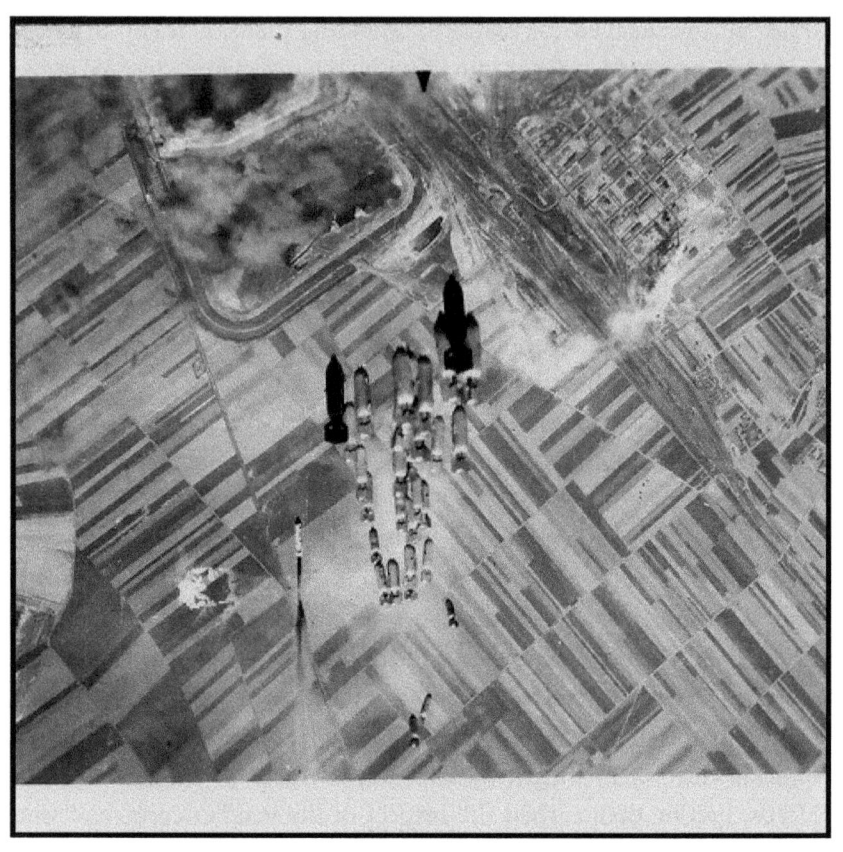

"Bomb Bay, Bombs Away." (Courtesy of 384thBombGroup.com)

1944 Missions

7

One group commander in the Eighth Air Force had advised his crews to consider themselves dead already. Perhaps if one could do this there would be no fear, but I couldn't bring myself to accept such a final solution.
— Col. Dale O. Smith

The new year of 1944 brought with it worsened weather conditions, such that the 384th ran fewer missions throughout January, and the Allison/Small crew flew only two missions for the entire month. The first mission for their crew was on January 5th aboard *Dynamite Express*, with the port area of Kiel, Germany as the Primary Target. Along at tail gunner was Sgt. Alfred A. Clark, subbing for the still hospitalized Kenneth Hougard. The 384th was the Lead Group and the weather at the target was "CAVU" (Ceiling and Visibility Unlimited), which meant they had a very good chance to achieve great bombing results. The Germans attempted a smokescreen to obscure the target, which was ineffective, allowing a successful attack on the target. Despite ball turret gunner Vernon Kaufman reporting lots of flak and enemy fighters, the 384th didn't have a single ship shot down.

Bombs Away

The introduction of the P-51 Mustang in early 1944 started making a huge difference in protecting the heavy bomber groups, so the mission schedule got dialed back up in a big way, leading eventually into "Big Week" in late February. The 384th, and indeed the Eighth Air Force as a whole, was about to have one of its busiest months yet. Perhaps the foul weather at the beginning of the year and the reduced number of missions were helpful, because they allowed for more time to bring the P-51 online and into the fight.

The new year also brought about a change in leadership for the Eighth Air Force. In January 1944, Lt. Gen. James "Jimmy" Doolittle, of the Tokyo Raid fame, took command of the Eighth Air Force, and implemented a very unpopular new policy. He sent orders down from his headquarters at Pinetree stating that "starting immediately, all combat crews would fly thirty combat missions instead of the previous twenty-five before being rotated…home." This change from the "brass;" had a big negative impact on morale, because the twenty-five-mission mark

The *Screaming Eagle* was one of Col. Dale O. Smith's frequently flown Forts, and the title of his memoirs.
(Courtesy of 384thBombGroup.com)

1944 Missions

was already thought of as very difficult and maybe even impossible to achieve by many of the men, given the high rate of losses in 1943. From *One Last Look*, Philip Kaplan talks about missions and longevity; "In 1943 and 1944, the average life of an Eighth Air Force bomber and crew was fifteen missions. The assigned tour of duty for crew members, however, was twenty-five missions, and out of this grew a set of odds most discouraging to anyone interested in longevity." The twenty-five-mission requirement was already very difficult for the men to obtain, and crew morale reflected it.

The new rule, announced on March 7, 1944, upping the mission requirement to thirty, gave pro-rata credit to men who were at or close to the previous mark of twenty-five. Herb Small had seventeen missions at that point and was awarded credit for one additional mission to make eighteen, so he then had to complete twelve more missions to make thirty, rather than eight more to make twenty-five. The change came ostensibly because losses were down due to the successful introduction of the P-51 Mustang. Plus, the big push was on to finish off the Luftwaffe before the eventual D-Day invasion could take place. The news was not received well by the men, and rule changes of this nature were part of the inspiration for the famous novel *Catch-22*, by Joseph Heller, which features a fictional Bomb Group stationed in Italy during World War II.

The poor weather conditions in January led to several delayed or scrubbed missions. Contrary to what those unfamiliar with combat missions might believe, the stress caused by repeated delays takes a physical and emotional toll on the men nearly as extreme as the missions themselves. In *First of the Many*, in an incredible first-hand eyewitness account, a photographer imbedded with the Eighth Air Force, John R. McCrary describes the incredible stress of delays on a particularly dangerous mission:

"At the end of thirty minutes, engines whined and peevishly coughed and angrily roared all over the field again. There was no scrub. There was no laughter now. We taxied a little further out from our hard standing, only about twenty yards. And then, once more, the engines choked and died. Once more there was a flash: 'Delay thirty minutes.'

Bombs Away

"At first there was relief. Now, surely, the mission would be scrubbed. But then the relief was routed by fresh nerve-strain. Each delay only snafus all the carefully worked out plans for attacks — further loosens the timing of the diversions and fighter escort — bet the Jerries know what we are cooking up by now — bet they'll be waiting. Yep, fears were fulfilled. At the end of thirty minutes, the same routine: Engines whine, cough, roar. And the taxiing begins again. Once more the engines die. This is too much. Nerves snap. Rich cussing crackles over the intercom through the ship. This time, the zero hour is delayed two hours. By now, the navigator has made so many changes on his forms that he can't figure out exactly when the take-off will be."

The second mission for the Allison/Small crew in January was not until January 21st, but the 384th flew several missions during that time, so I'm uncertain as to why their crew was not called upon to fly. Perhaps they were given some time for leave away from the base, their Fortress was under repair or they were simply fortunate. Though their "usual plane" was *Little Barney*, they by no means flew exclusively on her; Herb Small only recorded five total missions with *Little Barney*, and the crew's five missions prior to the January 21st mission aboard *Stella* were all flown on different Fortresses. *Little Barney* did indeed need extensive repairs due to damage caused by the December 13th aborted mission that ended in a crash landing.

> **[A check of the 384th's mission records shows that *Little Barney* did not fly for over two months following the unsuccessful mission of December 13, 1943, when the Allison/Small crew were forced to abort due to low oil pressure and an engine on fire. The aircraft was sidelined for extensive repairs and waiting for replacement parts to be available. *Little Barney* did not fly again until February 20, 1944, when once again, Earl Allison and Herb Small were in the cockpit.]**

1944 Missions

The January 21st mission, the eighth mission for Herb, was the second shot the 384th would take at knocking out the so-called "Nob-all" targets, which was the code term used for the German V-1 rocket launch sites that were scattered throughout France, Germany and the Netherlands. A V-1 launch site consisted of an inclined ramp roughly fifty yards long, protected from bombing on either side by earthen and concrete walls. The 27-foot winged V-1 "Flying Bombs," armed with almost 2,000 pounds of high explosives, were laid upon the ramp and propelled into the air at nearly 200 miles per hour toward London, reaching speeds as high as 400 mph before running out of fuel and crashing down on the streets of the city. At the peak of these attacks, roughly 100 "Buzz Bombs" per day were being thrown indiscriminately at the city, with a total of 9,521 in all. It was critical, as much for the sake of the citizens of London as for the all-around war strategy, that these bombs be stopped, either in the air or before they could be launched.

The 384th had been part of an earlier raid on these sites on the Normandy coast about sixty-five miles to the south of Calais in Le Meillard a week earlier, but the results were less than optimal The January 21st mission was a second run at another Noball site thirty miles to the southwest of the previous target. Ball turret gunner Vernon Kaufman wrote about the mission, for which waist gunners James Grimmett and William Kouski were grounded for reasons not known to me: "We were sweating out the oil pressure on number 3 engine. Then all of a sudden, we started throwing oil out of number 2, so we feathered it. We still made two passes over the target on three engines. We only saw a few bursts of flak and no fighters. Made it back o.k., we had a P-47 escort all the way. Boy did those fighters look good up there."

> **["Feathering" a damaged or inoperable engine meant rotating the propellers until the edges of the blades were pointed directly into the wind so that they would not spin due to the force of the air flowing over them. If the propellers were not feathered, they would spin erratically and cause large vibrations throughout the**

Merrie Hell

Crew of *Nuttall's Nut House*: Standing L-to-R: James Merritt; Earl Mason; Arthur Drogue; Alfred Nuttall; Randolph Jacobs. Kneeling L-to-R: Lawrence Wager; Edward O'Leary; Robert Compton; Jack Goetz; Alan Purdy
(Courtesy of 384thBombGroup.com)

plane, which could cause further damage to the engine and the rest of the plane.]

The Group Flight Leader for the mission was Major Alfred Nuttall aboard *Nuttall's Nut House*, with the Allison/Small crew flying in his group, with two squadrons of nine Forts on this relatively short run. With Herb and Earl for this mission, subbing in at the waist gunner positions on *Stella*, were experienced gunners Lawrence M. Hall and John Narog, with ten and eight missions to their credit respectively. Nuttall's group of nine was able to attack their Preuseville target and put their bombs on it to good results. A separate group of sixteen aircraft, led by Major George W. Harris, was not so fortunate, as cloud cover obscured their target, and despite making seven bomb runs, they were forced to return to base with their bomb load still onboard. Although the bomb-

1944 Missions

ing results were once again mixed, the 384th lost no aircraft on the January 21st mission, which had to feel like a small victory in and of itself to these men, who had seen so many of their brothers in arms lost.

It was almost two weeks more before the Allison/Small crew saw action again on February 3rd, which started a string of four missions in four days, striking at targets in Germany and France, including Luftwaffe training bases and an aircraft parts factory. The February 3rd mission aboard *Little Audrey* was fraught with issues from the outset, starting with waist gunner William Kouski passing out on the way up to join the formation, forcing the plane to return to base to drop him off and pick up substitute gunner Staff Sgt. William L. Harper. They took off again to join the mission, but after they crossed over the enemy coast, they were forced to turn back again and abort because the number two supercharger went out. Once again, every Fortress made it back to Grafton-Underwood, so there was a silver lining to be found, and Herb and the crew were given mission credit for the effort. But they certainly must have felt disappointed that they weren't able to participate in the raid with the rest of their Group.

The men didn't have to wait very long for another chance to fight, because the 384th was right back at it the next day, making a run at an aircraft parts factory in Frank am Main, Germany. Unfortunately, their previous mission's bad luck seemed to be sticking around; even though they were on yet another B-17 -- *Mr. Five by Five* -- they once again had to abort near the coast of France because of supercharger trouble. Fortunately, they were still given mission credit, bringing Herb's total number of missions to ten.

One has to wonder if the suddenly increased number of missions in February...seven missions in eleven days...was taking a toll on the already overworked ground maintenance crews, and if the Forts were having more issues than usual from the extra wear and tear. Even though Herb's crew didn't make it to the bombing run, they still went through all of the steps of prepping, both mentally and physically, for those two aborted missions, and endured much of the strain and stress that went with them.

The next two missions on February 5th and 6th gave them a chance to shake the bad luck, and they took it. With Kouski still sidelined, Staff Sgt. Angelo A. LaSalle subbed in at waist gunner on February 5th and Staff Sgt. Leland R. Smith, Jr. subbed in on February 6th (both missions being flown on *Shack Rabbit*) and headed for targets near Orleans, France. For both missions, the crew was also missing their stalwart navigator Lt. Sam Gardner, but it is unclear as to why he wasn't with them. Once again, ball turret gunner Vernon Kaufman had a bird's eye view from his post and gave a great description of the January 5th bombing results: "We were flying along very peacefully, when we were on the I.P. [Initial Point for the bombing run] and the bomb bay doors started to open. A second later it was bombs away. I could see the bombs hit the airfield and the target was completely in ruins. On our way back we flew about 10 miles east of Paris. The flak over Paris was so heavy that the blue sky was black as coal. We had a very good fighter escort that day and no enemy fighters were seen."

> **[Again, I have such wonderful words from Staff Sgt. Vernon Kaufman because of the generosity and kindness of his sister, Mrs. Donna Wiley. She was kind enough to share a copy of his personal mission diary — a treasured part of her family's history — with me, a novice writer and stranger more than 350 miles away.]**

February 20th brought the next mission for the Allison/Small crew after two weeks of inactivity and hopefully some well-earned rest, and it reunited them with their old friend, *Little Barney*, freshly back from repairs and maintenance. Now that he was twelve missions in, I wonder if Herb Small was a superstitious man, pondering "unlucky number thirteen" as he went through his pre-flight checklist with Earl Allison beside him. Whether he was or wasn't, the crew was on its way back up, with Sam Gardner back in the navigator position and Staff Sgts.

1944 Missions

John J. Stevens and Lawrence H. Wager at the waist gunner positions, replacing the still-grounded Grimmett and Kouski. Both were familiar faces, with Lawrence Wager having flown with Herb on Herb's first two missions with the Jacobs crew, and John Stevens from the February 4th mission just a couple of weeks earlier.

A major focus for James Doolittle was "Big Week," which began on February 20th. "Big Week" was Jimmy Doolittle's strategic vision, and for it the Eighth's focus turned to aggressively targeting and eliminating the German fighter planes and aircraft production industry in preparation for D-Day. The objective was to completely annihilate the Luftwaffe so that the Allies could have clear skies and uncontested airspace for the D-Day invasion. For the February 20th mission, 800 "heavies" (B-17 Flying Fortresses and B-24 Liberators) were assembled and sent to destroy aircraft industry targets in Germany. Part of the strategy was to attack the industrial targets on the ground, such that the damage would slow or stop fighter production. The other part was to purposely engage the Luftwaffe fighters, so they could be shot down. And in order to get the fighters in the air, they essentially used the heavy bombers as bait. If the bombers were attacking, they knew the German fighters would be in the air defending. The Eighth made sure the bombers were accompanied by large numbers of our fighters, including the newly added and vastly superior P-51 Mustang.

In the book *Jimmy Stewart: Bomber Pilot*, by Starr Smith, the author comments on Big Week; "The Germans were persistent in their efforts to get to the bombers, and paid in their most precious asset: experienced, valuable pilots." In the same book, he quotes air power historian Dr. Wesley Newton: "They lost their aces, their formation and unit leaders…The Germans, in spite of the damage to their aircraft factories, could still replace their fighter aircraft. But they could not replace the experience of veteran pilots and leaders."

Big Week meant five missions in six days for Herb's crew and the 384th as a whole. They were being called on to accomplish a critical goal...a goal that would, if achieved, make an enormous contribution to the war effort overall: **eliminate the Germany's ability to wage the air war.** It would especially contribute to the advantage in air power the Allies would eventually enjoy on D-Day. The first day's mission aboard the crew's beloved *Little Barney* on February 20th produced solid bombing results for the 384th, as they were able to bomb visually because of light cloud cover and put their bombs on the target. It was a good start for Big Week.

For Day 2, another pair of "borrowed" gunners were in the waist for a run at a fighter field and aircraft storage depot in Werl, Germany.

Jeter Crew: 546th Bomber Squadron: Back L-to-R: William Bailey; Sydney R. Jeter, Jr.; George F. Schultz, Jr.; Kenneth J. Swanson; Front L-to-R: Metro Persoskie; Edger A. Scheffer; John R. Liechtenstein; George Dupuis; Nelson Bishop; Ferdinand J. Madl; Donald V. MacDonald. (Courtesy of 384thBombGroup.com)

Staff Sgts. James J. Fisher and George Ursta were both seasoned veterans by that point and would have been welcomed additions to any crew. The mission of January 21, 1944 was George Ursta's 25th and final mission, and his last official duty date was February 25, 1944. (The increase of the mission goal to thirty hadn't happened yet.) He was headed home. The

1944 Missions

second day of Big Week didn't go quite as well as the first, because the targets were socked in with clouds, so the 384th contingent was forced to reverse course and seek targets of opportunity. They wound up attacking targets in Lingen, Germany, about seventy-five miles north of the original target and more or less on their way home. Once again, all the aircraft that went out on the Day 2 raid on Werl made it back to Grafton-Underwood.

With Day 3 of Big Week came a mission to bomb an aircraft factory in Halberstadt and Aschersleben, Germany. William Kouski was still out, replaced by Lawrence M. Hall once again, who had subbed in at waist gunner a few weeks earlier. There were two formations supplied by the 384th for this mission, but one -- the High Group of the Wing, led by Alfred Nuttall and Randall Jacobs in *Nuttall's Nut House* -- was forced to abort and turn back when it lost its formation due to thick cloud coverage during assembly. The Low Group was able to make it to the target and drop their bombs, but heavy smoke from the target area made assessing the damage difficult. The good luck of the 384th did not hold out, though; the group suffered the loss of five Fortresses on the mission.

The five losses were a heavy blow to the 384th. The group was set upon by a group of ten to fifteen Messerschmidt 109s and were hit with heavy flak barrages; four of the five losses occurred over Germany or the Netherlands. The good news, unbeknownst to the men at Grafton-Underwood at the time, was that of the 40 men of those four crews, only three were killed that day. The rest of the thirty-seven men aboard those ships were able to bail out and parachute to the relative safety of captivity by the Germans and spent the remainder of the war as POWs. Ships piloted by 2nd Lt. Norman F. DeFrees, 2nd Lt. William J. Kew, 1st Lt. Henry V. Markow and 2nd Lt. Raymond L. McDonald were those who "Failed to Return." The men who were not able to parachute to safety were 2nd Lt. William J. Kew and Staff Sergeant William J. Ross from *Clean Cut*, and co-pilot 2nd Lt. Paul M. Smith, Jr. of the McDonald crew aboard an unnamed B-17.

The fifth plane lost was part of an all-too-familiar tragedy of a

Bombs Away

mid-air collision during the take-off and assembly stage of the mission. Pilot 2nd Lt. Sydney R. Jeter, Jr.'s Fort *June Bug*, named after Jeter's wife June McClure Jeter, collided with another aircraft — (*Hells Angels*) from the 303rd Bomber Group out of Molesworth — during formation. The collision sheared the tail off of *Hell's Angels*, with only one man of that crew able to bail out and parachute down over England. Of Lt. Jeter's crew, only navigator 2nd Lt. William E. Bailey and bombardier 2nd Lt. Kenneth J. Swanson were able to parachute to safety. The nine others aboard *Hell's Angels* and eight others aboard Jeter's *June Bug* were tragically killed that day, a terrible loss for both bomber groups.

Big Week was very hard on the men of the 384th, and indeed the Eighth Air Force as a whole. In *Castles in the Air*, by Martin W. Bowman, a pilot from the 388th Bomb Group, 1st Lt. Lowell H. Watts, described the fatigue experienced by the men: "Now the strain began to tell. We'd done a lot of combat flying during the week and we were beginning to feel its effects. [Co-pilot Robert M.] Kennedy and I began trading off on the flying. Both of us were so tired that after about 15 minutes we just couldn't hold formation. Never in all my missions had I reached the stage where I was absolutely too tired to fly, but I reached it on this raid."

> **[A brief aside on my part, as I express what has been a growing frustration during my time of researching this biographical work and learning a great deal about the men and missions of the Eighth Air Force. I cannot help but think of how many men may have been needlessly sacrificed by the Higher Command making the decisions to send men out on missions in dangerous weather conditions, with little to no sleep and obvious combat fatigue. How many men were lost due to human error caused by simple fatigue? How many were lost due to mechanical malfunction because ground crews, similarly fatigued, were given only a few hours to patch planes up and send them**

1944 Missions

> back out? How many of these decisions, being made by men who had never set foot aboard a B-17 Flying Fortress or B-24 Liberator, were made to inflate their own egos and to be able to report "big gains" in the war to their superiors or the newspapers? How many could have been avoided by giving the men a decent night's sleep?]

But the men of the 384th, the way true frontline fighting men always seem to do, pushed through, because that's what men of that caliber (pun absolutely intended) do. The 384th had one day off on February 23rd and then Earl, Herb and the boys were back at it for two more missions aboard *Little Barney* to finish up Big Week. Staff Sgt. William Kouski was spelled for these last two mission by Staff Sgts. William L. Harper and Leland R. Smith, Jr. on the 24th and 25th of February respectively. Only one ship in the 384th was lost during these last two missions; *Mr. Five by Five*, piloted by 2nd Lt. Jack K. Larsen, which crash-landed near Bruchsal, Germany, on the 25th with all 10 men aboard surviving to be taken prisoner by the Germans.

The mission of February 24th showed them that sometimes luck, fate or perhaps the hand of God was on their side from time to time. The Sortie Report (#1880) shares the following details about the bombing run on this mission to bomb a ball-bearing factory in the infamous (to the Eighth Air Force, at least) city of Schweinfurt, Germany, when the Germans attempted to obscure the target with a smokescreen. "A smokescreen did not hide the target very well, and, in fact, helped the bombardiers identify and confirm the target location!" The key detail that is left out of that summary is that, according to the more detailed official after-action reports, the smokescreen was pushed around by winds over the target area such that it formed into an enormous arrow which happened to be pointing directly at the target!

Despite the heavy toll in men and aircraft during Big Week, the raids were getting results, and had delivered a very heavy blow to the enemy's ability to make aircraft and put them in the air. In *Blood and*

One of the *Berlin First* photos not in Life Magazine. Herb Small is standing in the middle in the white scarf. (Courtesy of 384thBombGroup.com)

Fears, Kevin Wilson discusses the subject: "The attacks of Big Week forced a desperate dispersal of the Reich's aircraft production, which finally put paid to German Air Ministry dreams of 5,000 fighters a month. The splitting of production centers would eventually make the supply lines fatally fragile to the might of the Allies' later Transportation Plan campaign. Big Week by no means finished the Luftwaffe, but it was the beginning of the end for Goering's force."

The Allison/Small crew had one more mission on February 28th to end the month, for which waist gunner William Kouski finally returned to the ship. For the first time since January 21st, after Kouski missing nine missions, the full crew -- including The Bills -- was back together and headed back to Preuseville, France to bomb V-1 Launch Site, this time once again aboard *Shack Rabbit*. There was heavy cloud cover so they were unable to visually verify their targets, which was absolutely required when a target was in occupied territory, so no bombs were

1944 Missions

dropped by the 384th on that mission. One crew aboard *Liberty Run*, piloted by 2nd Lt. Austin D. Rinne, went down in France during a bombing run after what they believed was mechanical failure of some kind aboard the plane, because no flak or fighters had been seen. All men aboard were able to bail out and parachuted down to become POWs, except for tail gunner Sergeant Charles T. Regan, whose chute failed to open after bailing out.

The month of February, to that point in the war, had the most missions performed by the 384th in a single month, with twelve missions besting the previous high of ten missions in December of 1943. Given that February is a short month, Command was really packing on the missions. There was no let-up in sight for March, with the Group sent out on a total of seventeen missions. The Allison/Small crew went out on ten of the twelve in February and seven of the seventeen in March, with most of the missions aimed at the heart of the German war-making industry, going after aircraft assembly plants, parts production and ball bearing production. The Eighth Air Force also had a new and daring target in mind for March: Berlin, the capital of Nazi Germany.

On March 3rd and March 4th, the 384th joined up with other elements of the Eighth Air Force for two unsuccessful attempts on Berlin. On the 3rd, the mission was recalled due to a shortage of fuel caused by having to maneuver excessively in response to poor weather. (The crews were given Combat Mission Credit for their efforts, however the Allison/Small crew did not receive credit, because they were forced to abort shortly after taking off due to problems with the supercharger again, this time on *Loose Goose*.).

On the 4th, once again bad weather caused problems for the mission right from the start. From the 384th Sortie Report (#2008): "The 384th Bombardment Group (H) flew as the Low Group of the 41st Combat Wing on today's mission. The Group had difficulty attaining its position in the wing formation because the wing leader used speeds greater than SOP [Standard Operating Procedure], finally catching up near the Ruhr Valley. With the ground completely obscured by dense cloud cover, the wing commander informed his formation that they would bomb a target of opportunity (TOO), initially thought to be Cologne (Köln), Germany, but later determined to be Bonn."

As the saying goes, "The Third Time's the Charm." On March 6th, the 384th joined up once again with a larger force from the Eighth, attempting to add twenty-five Forts to fly with the 40th Composite Combat Wing and the 41st Composite Combat Wing. Due to difficulties in assembly, twenty of the twenty-five ships had to abort and return to base. Among the five who stayed in the air and made the historic run to Berlin was the Allison/Small crew aboard the Fort *Goin' Dog*, with the full complement of their original crew to be part of the distinct honor. This first mission to Berlin -- to finally strike a blow at the heart of the enemy -- was so important for the war effort and for morale back home that it was featured in a multi-page spread of the March 27, 1944 issue of *Life Magazine*, with a grand picture of the men who completed the mission posing on and around a B-17 appropriately named *Berlin First*.

As Briefed made very specific mention of the success and excitement of the first successful raid on Berlin: "The 544th was the first of our squadrons to get over Berlin. Fifty men in five airplanes piloted by Lieutenant Earl T. Allison, James E. Foster, Donald S. Morrison, George B. West, and John E. Clayton." "By the time interrogation was over it had been a sixteen-hour working day for the men who went to Berlin, and they were all a little tired. But they talked about it over a hot supper that had been kept waiting for them in the mess halls, and they talked about it afterward in the clubs, and they talked about it in the barracks after the lights had been turned off.

"Now that the jinx was broken, the 384th was to make many trips to the German capital."

The 384th saw a lot of action in March of 1944, hitting Berlin once more on March 8th, as well as other targets of industry the rest of the month throughout Germany and V-1 rocket sites throughout France. They also lost ten more Forts in the month of March. Thankfully, many of the men who were on those Forts were able to parachute to safety or survive by ditching or crash-landing in various locations, so the toll in

1944 Missions

April 9, 1944 Mission Crew: L to R standing: Arthur Drogue, Jr; Jack Nagel; Dale O. Smith; Earl Allison; Herbert Small; Joseph Cittadini. In front: William Laubenstein; Kenneth Hougard; Vernon Kaufman; William Clements; James Grimmett.
(Courtesy of 384thBombGroup.com)

lives lost wasn't as bad as it could have been.

Navigator Lt. Sam Gardner was replaced on March 9th for the remainder of the crew's missions by Lt. Joseph L. G. Cittadini, who features prominently in a later chapter; the two men swapped crews, with Gardner moving to fly his final eleven missions mostly with 2nd Lt. Theodore Goller Jr.'s crew, which was Cittadini's original and regular crew. I have yet to find the reason for the switch, but it would work out to be an incredibly fortunate switch for Sam Gardner.

The Allison/Small crew flew a total of only seven missions in March, with two of those not counting for Mission Credit, which meant Herb's mission tally at the end of March was twenty-one; he would have only needed four more missions under the old "twenty-five missions" rule. He was awarded the Air Medal upon completion of his first five missions and received an Oak Leaf Cluster for each additional five missions completed after that, totaling three clusters by the end of March. I don't think medals and ribbons meant very much to most of the men in the 384th, or indeed the Eighth Air Force as a whole. The real "award"

Doasy Doats

Bombs Away

was to complete your missions, bring your Forts home safely and survive the war to get back home to your family and loved ones. A great example of that mentality is the William Laubenstein Purple Heart story in Chapter Five; the guy was so eager to get home to his wife and family that he didn't bother to take the time to pick up his medal. That's a mindset that probably gets harder to understand with each successive generation, I would venture, but it was common amongst these men.

Toward the end of March, after all of the heavy fighting they had seen, by way of Special Orders #54, dated March 21, from Col. Dale O. Smith, Earl Allison, Herbert Small and Jack Nagel were granted a 7-day sick leave to begin on or about March 23rd. They were presumably -- though I haven't been able to confirm it -- sent to what was called a "Flak House," or an "Officers Rest Home" in order to get some much needed and deserved Rest and Relaxation away from aerial combat. Flak Houses were an assortment of stately English manor homes that had been converted into luxury hotel and recreation facilities, offering all sorts of amenities and activities for officers needing a break from the action. Any time away from the Air Force's version of the front lines was critical for the mental health and wellbeing of the men, though many of them became frustrated by and resentful of the time away. To them it meant that they were tucked safely away from the action, while other men were flying missions in their place, putting themselves in danger. These were a different breed of young men, and the bonds that they formed with each other are beyond what most of us now can even imagine.

April started off slowly for the 384th, with a week and a half layoff from missions due to poor weather over England and most of Europe; the weather had to have been incredibly bad for them to not be flying during that span of time, because it took a lot for missions to be scrubbed or even postponed, much less to not even be scheduled in the first place. They had sent formations up into some horrendous weather conditions numerous times throughout 1943 and 1944, so to not even schedule missions meant the weather had to have been at its very worst. The break in action had to have come as both a relief and possibly a

1944 Missions

source of renewed anxiety for the men.

The first mission in April for the 384th (number 86) didn't come until the 9th, when Earl Allison would welcome the base commander Col. Dale O. Smith into the pilot's seat of *Nuttall's Nut House*, as well as an additional navigator in 2nd Lt. Arthur J. Drogue Jr. The mission would also see co-pilot Herb Small shifted to the tail gunner position for the second time. This was done because of Col. Smith's policy requiring an experienced pilot to fly in the tail gunner position when he (Smith) was flying the lead plane. It meant that an experienced pilot could evaluate the tightness of the formation, for which Col. Smith was an absolute stickler. Having a second navigator onboard when he was flying lead was also a policy of Col. Smith, to ensure accuracy of the route when the entire formation was depending on them to lead the way.

A typical scene of the men on and around the control tower at Grafton-Underwood anxiously awaiting the return of Forts from a bombing mission.
(Courtesy of 384thBombGroup.com)

Elise

Bombs Away

"BERLIN FIRST" In this colossal portrait one Flying Fortress and some 130 young men commemorate an historic moment in the life of the U. S. Eighth Air Force. The men are the crews of a single formation of heavy bombers which on March 4 made the first American attack on Berlin.

The airplane is named *Berlin First*, not only because it took part in the raid, but also because all but one of its crew flew to Berlin on their first flight over the Continent.

In addition to being the record of a milestone, this

34

"Berlin First" *Life Magazine* spread. It's hard to tell, but I believe part of the Allison/Small crew are in the top left portion of this picture, inlcuding Jack Nagel, William Clements and Aurthur Drogue.

The first paragraph of the article reads: "In this colossal portrait one Flying Fortress and some 130 young men commerorate an historic moment in the life of the U.S. Eighth Air Force. The men are the crews of a single formation of heavy bombers which on March 4* made the first American attack on Berlin. The airplane is named *Berlin First,* not only because it took part in the raid, but also because all but one of its crew flew to Berlin on their first flight over the Continent."

1944 Missions

> picture partly overcomes a curious anonymity which has obscured the fliers of the Eighth. For men who are making one of the greatest American offensive efforts of the war, little has been told of them. Only their heroes are known to the U.S. The *Berlin First* portrait is also a brief reminder of the human scale of the war in the air. The tight good-sized group of men shown above is just about enough to fly 13 heavy bombers.
>
> The first raid was nearly forgotten in the great Berlin attacks which came in the week after March 4. The raid of March 6, in which 800 Fortresses and Liberators cascaded 2,000 tons of bombs on the city, was another precedent for the Eighth. For the first time American daylight bombers had equaled the most ambitious of RAF attacks. For Berlin destruction, turn the page.

I believe Earl Allison and Herb Small are standing on the wing just right of center to the right of the propellor...Herb is in a lighter-colored jacket.

The article continues: "In addition to being the record of a milestone, this picture partly overcomes a curious anonymity which has obscured the fliers of the Eighth. For men who are making one of the greatest American offensive efforts of the war, little has been told of them. Only their heroes are known to the U.S. The *Berlin First* portrait is also a brief reminder of the human scale of the war in the air. The tight good-sized group of men shown above is just about enought to fly 13 heavy bombers."

Chaplain's Office

Bombs Away

The mission was to Marienburg, Germany to attack a Focke-Wulfe assembly plant, and bad weather forced ten ships to turn back because of difficulty during formation assembly, meaning that only twenty-four of the thirty-five Forts that took off actually completed the mission. One B-17, piloted by 2nd Lt. George W. Schock, was hit by flak, causing its wing to catch fire. Its crew was all able to parachute out, with nine of the ten men captured by the Germans, and one man, engineer Tech. Sgt. Lucian G. Shannon, Killed in Action. However, it was still a successful mission, as described by the Sortie Report for mission #86: "However, clear weather over the continent and in the target area enabled a majority of the bombers to successfully attack their assigned target."

The losses had been relatively light during most of March and early April, but that was destined to change, on unlucky April the 13th, no less, when a mission to Schweinfurt, Germany would see nine Forts lost. Despite the overall mission result being a successful attack on the assigned target, ninety men would not return home to Grafton-Underwood on that terrible day. Twenty-six of the ninety men were Killed in Action, fifty-five were captured by the Germans and spent the remainder of the war in POW camps, and nine managed to evade capture with the help of the various underground groups that operated in occupied territory to help downed Allied airmen.

The beginning of 1944 had been a busy and productive time for the 384th and the Eighth Air Force as a whole. They were working hard and getting real results. The bombing results achieved in February, March and April of 1944 helped to give the D-Day forces air superiority and skies that were virtually free of Luftwaffe fighters and bombers on June 6th. The Eighth Air Force owned the sky over Normandy.

Herb Small sat out the next two missions flown by his crew (April 18th and 22nd), with Cap. Alfred Nuttall taking his place next to Earl Allison, though I do not know why. Cap. Nuttall brought along his usual navigator from his own crew in place of Joseph Cittadini, who had traded crews with Sam Gardner in March as mentioned earlier. Perhaps Nuttall simply liked his own guy being in charge of the maps, which is understandable, given Nuttall's record of missions and success in the

1944 Missions

384th. He was a recipient of the Distinguished Flying Cross and completed a full thirty missions. He was with the 384th for an impressive fourteen months, from June 1943 through August 1944, surviving some of the most difficult times for the Bomber Group and chalking up one of the most impressive records with thirty completed missions to his credit.

Sam Gardner, Herb's former navigator for seventeen missions, finished his twenty-ninth and last mission on April 19, 1944, and saw his last day of military duty on April 26, 1944. I believe he finished with only twenty-nine missions because of the pro-rated award of one additional mission credit from the rule change taking the mission requirement to thirty. The move of Sam Gardner to the crew of 2nd Lt. Theodore "Ted-

One of the more prolific bombers in the 384th, *Hell's Messenger*, with Major Maurice A. Booska (R) and his ground Crew Chief. Hell's Messenger was assigned to 151 missions in the 384th and earned Combat Mission Credit for 104 of them.

Hell's Messenger on a mission. (Courtesy of 384thBombGroup.com)

dy" Goller Jr., in exchange for Joseph Cittadini coming to the Allison/Small crew, proved literally a lifesaver for Gardner. He completed his last day of duty just one day before his friend Herb Small's fateful flight, and just a week and a half before what could have been his own.

No one had any idea what the mission the next day, on April 27, 1944...a supposed "Milk Run"...would bring, but it would change the lives of Herb's family for generations to come, as evidenced by his great-nephew -- me -- writing this biography.

---

* The *Life Magazine* article has the date of the successful Berlin raid as "March 4th," but all the records from the 384th BG show that the first successful Berlin raid occurred on March 6th. The March 4th attempt at Berlin was turned back due to heavy cloud coverage over the target.

Final Missions

8

> *"Direct hit by flak immediately after bombs away; fire started in cockpit and spread throughout aircraft, which peeled off to the left and started down and then exploded; no chutes observed; crashed 2 km w of Valognes, France."*
> - 384th BG Sortie Report #2787

The morning of April 27th was no different than two dozen mornings when Herb was woken up at the unGodly hour of 3:30, stumbling half-asleep to the bathroom to shave and shower, then taking his bike to the mess hall for breakfast...or maybe getting picked up by one of the shuttle trucks. Hot coffee and the treat of real eggs for mission days was something to look forward to, at least...if you had any appetite at that point. Five-time crewmember with Herb, navigator Joseph Cittadini, described one such morning: "My mind is still in a daze as I enter the brightly lighted mess. My briefcase and knapsack are silent sentinels at a chair while I get on the fresh egg line. Fresh eggs in Britain are a luxury. I guess they are hard to get back home, too. Personnel not slated to fly will eat powdered eggs if they want them, but most will settle for cereal. There are many tired looking new faces among the diners here this morning. I glance nervously around to try to locate a familiar face. A kind of panic wells up within me until I see one."

> [Cittadini had many eloquent passages like this in his brief war memoir, titled *20th Mission: a short account as well as my memory serves*, which I found in a Florida State University online library collection. I particularly like the phrase "my briefcase and knapsack are silent sentinels…" as he uses them to save himself a seat at the mess table. Another one I like is from a description of the view out his navigator's compartment window during a mission "…and all I see is clouds, white and fluffy and tinged with morning sunlight." I don't know if Cittadini wrote more than his story of his 20th mission, but I certainly think he had a knack for it.]

The Primary Target for the mission that day, which the 384th was flying as an independent Group without a Wing formation, was another site for German V-Weapons near Sottevast, France, a small agricultural area in the northern part of the Cotentin Peninsula, just south of Cherbourg. This was supposedly going to be a "Milk Run," the slang term for an easy and/or short mission that wasn't expected to see much resistance from German flak or fighters. It was also the first mission for which Lt. Herbert W. Small would be in the pilot's seat, commanding his crew, rather than the co-pilot's seat or the tail gunner's position. Only it wasn't his crew he was flying with that day. It was nine guys with whom Herb had never flown, aboard a Fort that had not yet been named…or even painted. That's about as "green" as it gets.

> [If you search "Sottevast v-2 bunker" on Google Maps, you can still see the remains of one of the sites they were going after. It's very interesting that

Final Missions

those are among the World War II remnants that still speckle the Normandy countryside.]

This was the crew with Herb for his twenty-seventh time going into battle -- although he only had official mission credit for twenty-two at that point due to a few aborted missions:

- 2nd Lt. Herbert W. Small — Pilot
- 2nd Lt. Roy J. Morris — Co-Pilot
- 2nd Lt. James E. McGue — Navigator
- 2nd Lt. John M. Sewack — Bombardier
- Staff Sgt. Marion L. Parker — Radio Operator
- Sgt. Richard D. Pirrello — Engineer/Top Turret
- Sgt. John B. Reynolds — Ball Turret Gunner
- Sgt. Edward J. Potkay — Tail Gunner
- Staff Sgt. David E. George — Waist (Flex) Gunner
- Sgt. Russell H. Ulrich — Waist (Flex) Gunner

Herb's B-17 crew of April 27, 1944. (Courtesy of the family.)

Eleanor Maureen

Bombs Away

[There have been a few heartbreaking moments for me in learning about my uncle and in writing this book, and I am compelled to share one that I discovered in writing this chapter. I knew that these were all men who were new to flying with Herbert Small, and that it was his first mission as the pilot, as opposed to co-pilot or tail gunner, but I didn't know much more about these new guys. When I dug deeper, I learned that all of them had been assigned to the 384th less than two weeks prior on April 16th, and with the exception of tail gunner Edward J. Potkay, who had one mission under his belt, it was the first mission for all of them. *Their very first mission.* They barely got a chance to be part of the story before their lives were violently cut short. But they are going to be part of *this* story.]

The Summary of Mission report for April 27, 1944 reads as follows: "Twenty-one (21) aircraft, including three (3) spares, of the 384th Bombardment Group (H) took off between 0811 and 0826 hours. Group assembly was accomplished without difficulty. There was no Wing assembly for this mission. The English Coast was departed at 1009 hours and the enemy coast was crossed at 1041 hours. Weather at the target was CAVU but hazy."

Things started out looking pretty good for the 384th's 96th mission. Seasoned veteran Earl Allison was leading the formation in *Nuttall's Nut House,* with Lt. Col. James R. Rembert Jr. in the co-pilot's seat and John Q. Curtin of Randolph Jacob's crew sitting below them at the navigator's desk. In his own Fort, first-time pilot Herb Small had his very green crew in formation directly behind and to the left of his friend Earl Allison's Fort. Herb's plane was a brand-new B-17G with no name and no nose art, shining brightly in the sun because it had not yet received a paint job. Some have argued that these bright, shiny new B-17s made altogether too tempting targets for both enemy flak and fighters.

Final Missions

They may have been right.

Aboard Earl Allison's ship *Nuttall's Nut House* on April 27th were the usual crew, plus a couple of new faces:

- Lt. Col. James R. DuBose, Jr. — Commander
- 2nd Lt. Earl T. Allison — Pilot
- 2nd Lt. John Q. Curtin — Navigator
- 2nd Lt. Jack C. Nagel — Bombardier
- T/Sgt. William F. Laubenstein — Radio Operator
- Staff Sgt. William A. Clements — Engineer/Top Turret
- Staff Sgt. Vernon H. Kaufman — Ball Turret Gunner
- 2nd Lt. Orion R. Allio — Tail Gunner
- Staff Sgt. Kenneth N. Hougard — Waist/Flex Gunner
- Staff Sgt. James H. Grimmett — Waist/Flex Gunner

The route was relatively direct and short, first heading southwest over England then leaving the English Coast above Weymouth, then due south for the Channel Islands of Guernsey and Jersey but turning southeast just before coming into range of the German guns placed there. Just after passing over the coastline of France, they turned to head almost directly north for the bombing run on Sottevast, which is about five miles inland just south of the strategically important port city of Cherbourg.

The Group had a relatively easy time of assembling the formation and enjoyed great visibility for most of the mission, so the men had every reason to feel confident they would have a good run. According to an after-action report by Lt. Col. James R. Dubose, Jr., who was sitting in Herb Small's usual seat on *Nuttall's Nut House*: "Bombs were away at 1051 hours from an altitude of 20,000 feet on a Mag. [magnetic] Heading of 011 degrees following a bomb run of 3 minutes." A three-minute bomb run was a pretty short one, which was likely a component that added to the men's belief that this was indeed a "Milk Run." However, any bombing run, from the Initial Point (IP) until Bombs Away, was arguably the most dangerous time for any bomber mission. When the pilot turned control of the plane over to the bombardier to start the

Bombs Away

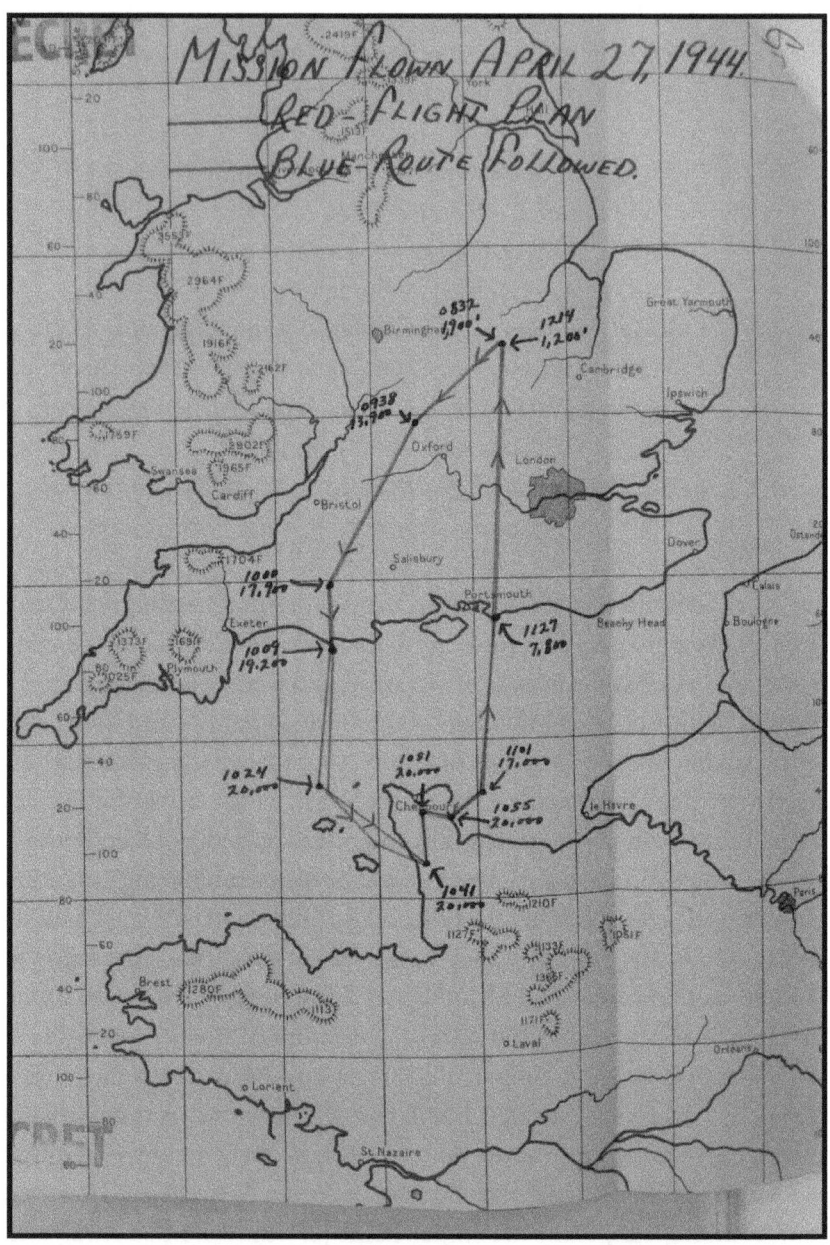

Map of the bombing route for April 27th. (Courtesy of 384thBombGroup.com.)

Final Missions

bombing run, every ship in the Group had to fly straight and true, with no change of course and no evasive maneuvering to avoid flak. They became sitting ducks for German flak gunners, who knew this about American bomber tactics, and would train several of their guns on one specific patch of sky just ahead of the group in a "barrage." The Germans knew the bombers had to fly straight and take what they were dishing out until they released their bombs.

Flak was universally hated among the bomber crews because they could do almost nothing at all about it, other than try to avoid it. At least with enemy fighters, they could fight back, even if sometimes the odds were stacked against them. Many gunners reported feeling much less fear during a mission when they were operating their guns and "giving some back" to the enemy. W.W. Ford, of the 92nd Bomb Group had this to say on the topic in *The Mighty Eighth War Manual*, by Roger A. Freeman: "You don't see any shell; you don't hear anything. You just see this little puff of smoke and then shortly after, it sounds like somebody is throwing gravel all over the airplane. You're fascinated by it. You know that it can hurt you very badly, but you're fascinated by it…you watch it. It's kind of like watching a snake."

T/Sgt. William F. Laubenstein, the usual radioman for the Allison/Small crew, who was also trained as a gunner, gave a description of the gunnery action in his memoirs: "At this time I was a waist gunner in the plane. The 50-cal. machine gun weighed about 65 lbs. and could fire 575 rounds per minute at a speed of 2900 feet per second. Every fifth round was a tracer, which helped the gunman to see how he was shooting and where to correct his aim, if necessary. The flak over Germany was heavier over military targets. A 37mm [enemy flak] cannon was dangerous up to 10,000 feet and an 88mm cannon was dangerous up to 40,000 feet. The bombs that we dropped were 100, 250, 500 and 1000 pounds in size."

[One question that keeps coming back to me is if it would have been beneficial to the 8th Air Force

to have the B-17s (and the other bombers) carry a slightly smaller bomb load in order to be able to devote more weight on the plane to additional armor plating strategically placed throughout the ship. Instead of carrying twelve 500-pound bombs, for a total bomb load weight of 6,000 pounds, perhaps they could have carried ten bombs, and been able to add 1,000 pounds' worth of armor...or eleven bombs and 500 pounds of armor...where it might protect the men. It seems that there could have been a substantial savings in human life in return for a fairly modest cost on the bomb delivery end.]

The Group had just released their bombs, following the lead of Earl Allison's bombardier, when Herb Small's plane, according to the reports, "suffered a direct hit by flak immediately after bombs away. A fire which started in the cockpit seemed to spread throughout the aircraft. The aircraft peeled off formation to the left and immediately started down. No 'chutes were observed leaving the aircraft." The left wing had been shot off, which very likely ignited some of the fuel that was stored in tanks in the wings, which maybe set the oxygen supply on fire, as well. That could explain why the fire spread so quickly throughout the plane. The quote above is from Sortie Report #2787 and Missing Air Crew Report #4350, and they are the words of Herb Small's friend Earl Allison, who was given the unfortunate task of writing the MACR after witnessing his friend's death.

As the plane pitched over to the left, it must have turned nearly 180 degrees to head south as it went down, because it wound up crashing close to Rocheville, which is a little more than a mile south of Sottevast. The crash was observed by many people in and around Rocheville, and in an article written by Carol (Parker) Schafer, the sister of radio operator Sgt. Marion L. Parker. She writes: "Some eyewitness on the ground stated that there were parachutes in the air, and that the escaping crewmen were killed by enemy gunfire as they floated to the ground. This is probably untrue and is well refuted by other eyewitnesses who say that all perished in the crash and that there were no chutes.

She continues: "There is a slight possibility that Marion actually survived the crash. A letter to his mother from the Air Corps states in part; 'He was taken to a Main Aid Station at Ste-Georges-d'Aunay, France, where he died.' They claim that this information was obtained when they translated 'several volumes of captured German records.' It is still difficult to state with certainty that he survived the crash, as information from Occupied Europe at that time was sketchy, and eyewitnesses claim to have seen no survivors."

The men aboard *Nuttall's Nut House* with Earl Allison, who had known Herb since training and flown twenty-plus missions with him, had to sit by and watch their friend and respected colleague plummet to the ground in flames. The crash site was described in the Missing Aircraft Report as "2 km west of Valognes near Le Pont Durand," however, Le Pont Durand is over four miles west (over seven km) of Valognes, which possibly speaks to the haze of battle and the vagaries of war that these distances were not consistent.

Ball turret gunner Vernon Kaufman, who would have had the best view of the crash from the belly of the plane, along with replacement tail gunner Orion R. Allio, shared his thoughts; "This raid turned out to be a very sad one, as our co-pilot Small was knocked down by flak. We were flying lead, and he was flying number three position, when all of a sudden, he peeled off and went down in flames. No parachutes came out. The flak was intense. The mission was short, but very rough to my estimation."

Just like that, ten brave men who had stepped up to heed the call to defend the nation and the people they loved were gone, shot down over a country that was not their own, in defense of people they had never met. Men from Pennsylvania, Colorado, Michigan, California, New York (City and State), Connecticut and Massachusetts. From towns even smaller than Sheffield all the way to the Big Apple of New York City, from West Coast to East Coast, these men came together to fight a common enemy. Just like that, their lives were ended, thousands of miles away from home and the ones they loved.

The Missing Air Crew Report has an interesting bit of mystery to it in the "Downing Report" page. It lists the "Disposition of the Crew" as "10 Men Dead." However, only nine of the ten men are listed. The tenth slot — where Herbert Small's name should appear — simply reads "Not Identified." The page after that lists the "Identification Tags" (dog tags) of the men recovered, and once again there are only nine names, with Herb's not on the list. A third document lists the initial place of burial of the crew at the English Cemetery in Cherbourg on April 29th, with Herb's name once again not among the others. There is a hand-written note on the document that mentions that the man listed as "Unknown" is likely Herbert W. Small. The men were only buried in Cherbourg temporarily, eventually being moved to their individual final resting places, Herb's being the American Cemetery in Normandy.

A possible answer to this apparent mystery was revealed to me by a cousin of mine, who knew this from her mother, Herb's sister Ann. Herb, for some unknown reason, didn't like to wear his Dog Tags. Perhaps it was a superstition reserved only for missions, or maybe he didn't like them generally and preferred to not wear them at all. They can be seen on his chest in at least one photo of him with his crew (the picture in Chapter Seven of the crew and *Nuttall's Nut House*), but maybe that wasn't the norm. Possibly the metal tags were at risk of freezing to a man's skin at the high altitudes if they were worn against bare skin, or they were just one more thing to get tangled up with the rest of the gear the men had to wear. Or perhaps the wise-beyond-his-years Herb realized that the Dog Tags, by their very existence, represented the ever-present possibility of severe injury or death to a soldier, sailor or airman, and wearing them was a subliminal acknowledgement by a man that those things could happen to him. Many of the airmen were superstitious, which is common among warriors, both on and above the battlefield, when they know there is only so much they themselves can do to influence the outcome, and perhaps an appeal to fate, luck or fortune needs to be made.

Final Missions

The original cemetery for fallen U.S. servicemen in Cherbourg. In the foreground, notice the graves of David E. George and John B. Reynolds, from the crew that crashed with Herb on April 27th. Courtesy of the Small family.)

*****

A very small silver lining to that terrible day was that the mission was reported as very successful, with the post-bombing pictures showing the area just north of the village of Sottevast as peppered with bomb craters. To this day, there are still the battered remains of a V-2 site just outside of Sottevast. I imagine that it would have been some small comfort to Herb, and possibly to his family at the time, that his final mission was counted as a success and that he was responsible for helping to take out weapons that were doing great damage in both property and lives in London. With any great loss, those grieving often cling to any positive point they can find, however small it may be.

The loss of Herb Small meant that Earl Allison had to write the promised letter back home to Herb's mother, with the dreaded "code words" incorporated into the text so as to not be edited out by the base's censors. Another of Herb's nephews, my cousin Stan, related the following story to me about his mother, who was Herb's sister Cece: "One night around the time Herb was Killed in Action, before they had received Earl Allison's letter, Mom [fifteen-year-old Cece] awoke with a start and had a premonition (vision?) of him standing at the foot of her bed. She swears he appeared to her, and he kept assuring her he was alright and there was nothing to worry about. A few days later they got the letter."

That certainly could have been the very vivid dream of a teenage girl terribly worried about her beloved big brother, but I'm in no position to discount or dispute the idea that it was indeed a premonition. It was real to her, whether it was a vision, apparition or dream, and that's all that matters. It was real enough to help her with the loss of her beloved brother at the time, and with her grief that lasted the remaining eighty years of her life.

The loss of Herb was certainly a blow to the Allison crew, who up until that point had not lost any of their original group. What thoughts must have gone through their minds? *If only he hadn't switched over to the other crew? Was it bad luck to fly with all those new guys? Was the new crew too inexperienced? Did they do something wrong? He would still be alive if he'd just stayed with us.* Survivor's guilt hits even harder when you're close to the ones who died, and when some odd circumstance changes the usual manner of things…like giving your flight away to a friend in need, and then his plane goes down.

Joseph Cittadini, the navigator who flew five missions with Herb and the crew, made specific mention of the loss of Herb Small in his memoirs *20th Mission,* when he described the morning of another mission just a few days later. "I get my eggs (sunny-side up) and return to my chair to eat. My eyes wander around the room picking out a few of the men I recognize. I dawdle over my breakfast with no enthusiasm — despite the fresh eggs. Powdered eggs were an abomination invented by some guy back in the States who, it seems, was doing his share to help Germany win the war. In my solitude, my brain recalls faces that should be here this morning. I become melancholy with the realization of how many close friends are missing. Jim Geary, our original co-pilot,

Final Missions

shot down on his seventh or eighth mission. Don't know if he's dead or trying to get out of Europe via the 'underground.' Fioretti, Bailey, Merlo, Griffiths, **Small**, Brookings, Big T and many more fine young men are gone now. As I think of them, I say a little prayer for them and their families. I'm feeling low and my mind is still clouded because of insufficient sleep."

The men of the Earl Allison crew felt the loss of one of their own in the death of Herbert Small, and they were probably feeling a whole range of emotions, including guilt-ridden relief that they hadn't shared the same fate; anger at their enemy and maybe even at the "higher-ups" who had sent them out on the supposed "milk run." Perhaps they feared that as their number of missions climbed, with most of them having twenty-plus to their credit at that point, that statistically they were pushing their luck. The seemingly impossible goal of twenty-five missions, that was then expanded to thirty missions in early 1944, had a very serious effect on the morale and psychological state of the men.

Earl Allison may have felt it more than anyone in the 384th. On April 28th, one day after his friend Herb was shot down, Earl wrote that dreaded letter to Herb's mother, Cecelia (Ford) Small, the great-grandmother I knew affectionately as "Nanny." I was shown this letter in one of my recent visits with Herb's last surviving sibling Mary – now Mary Ustico -- just months before she passed away at age 96 in 2024.

Earl wrote:

My Dear Mrs. Small,

I hardly know how to write you this letter and yet, if I am not greatly mistaken, your womanly intuition told you the moment you saw the envelope that this letter would bear sad news. Perhaps you have already received the dreaded War Dept. telegram telling you that Herbie is missing in action.

Herb — we knew him as "Squire" during these many months together — had been checked out as a first pilot, and was flying with a crew of his own. He was flying next to my *plane and doing a fine, fine job, for Herb was a good pilot. Well, Mrs. Small, I'm sure I don't understand why these things happen, it could have been any of us in the formation; in fact, my own plane received several hits, but Herb's plane suffered an unlucky one, and it went down. I can scarcely bring myself to say it, but perhaps at least it will bring you endless anxiety*, for it just doesn't seem possible to me yet. I am sorely afraid that the worst has happened.*

I do so wish I could have been able to write more optimistically, Mrs. Small, but I know you would want the truth.

"Squire" was a good young man, Mrs. Small. As you know I knew him intimately, and you are justly proud of a fine son. We fellows in this nasty business do not "kid" ourselves — we aren't heroes, but are just doing a job that we don't like but a job that simply must be done. And Herb did his job 100% — And I know. Yes, he was a real part of me.

If and when I get home once more from this mess I would very much like to visit you. Herb and I always had a standing invitation to visit each other's home in good old Massachusetts.

*[I believe Earl Allison may have misspoken here, meaning to write "perhaps at least it will bring an end to your endless anxiety," or something similar. I also do not know the origin of the nickname "Squire." In Allison's letter is the only place I've seen it.]

Not long after his letter was sent, Earl Allison flew his own final mission, and his mother would soon receive her own War Department telegram...probably before his letter to Herb's mother had been delivered.

Eleven days after Herb was shot down, on May 8th, the Earl Allison crew shook themselves out of bed at the usual unGodly hour,

Final Missions

Insignia patch of the 384th Bombardment Group.

plodded to the showers, latrines and mess hall, just as they had so many times before, and finally filed into the briefing room. They had just the day before learned of the loss of another aircraft, with the fate of another buddy unknown. Navigator 2nd Lt. Joseph L.G. Cittadini, flying with his usual pilot, 2nd Lt. Theodore "Ted" Goller, had crash landed near Schweinburg, Germany, on a mission to Berlin. All ten of Goller's crew survived the crash and were taken prisoner by the Germans, spending the rest of the war as POWs. However, back at the base, the fate of men who were shot down was usually not known for weeks, months or even until the end of the war. And sometimes not at all.

Flak Hopper

Bombs Away

It was from this common phenomenon that the motto of the 384th — **Keep the Show on the Road** -- was born. In Major General Dale O. Smith's memoir, *Screaming Eagle*, he describes the origin of the beloved motto: "Before my time with the 384th, the well-liked air exec, Lt. Col. Selden L. McMillin, had gone down on a mission, and after several weeks a postcard arrived from a POW camp in Germany. It was from McMillen and he wrote, "Let's keep the show on the road." This motto caught on like wildfire and became a part of the group insignia."

The Allison crew learned in the briefing that their mission would have them headed back to Sottevast, France, where they had so recently seen their friend Herb shot down the last time they went up for a mission. I can only imagine the groans and gritting of teeth that must have filled the room when the curtain was drawn back from the map in the front of the room to reveal nearly the exact same target for the mission. In place of Herb in the co-pilot's seat was the very experienced Randolph Jacobs, the first pilot Herb had flown missions with upon his arrival at Grafton-Underwood. Jacobs brought along with him his navigator 1st Lt. John Q. Curtin, because Allison's usual navigator Sam Gardner had completed his missions back on April 19th and was headed home. And Cittadini, who had been filling in at navigator for the last five missions, had gone down the day before. Given that the crew had experienced so much loss recently, they must have had some misgivings about heading back to the fateful Sottevast.

The 384th was flying in the High Group, with bombers from the 303rd and 379th in Lead and Low Group respectively. It was the second mission flown by the 384th that day, in a month when they saw a lot of missions out of Grafton-Underwood. Conditions were once again "CAVU" (Ceiling and Visibility Unlimited) at the target, and the Group was lined up behind Allison's *Reno's Raider* for the bombing run, aiming to take out more of the V-1 rocket sites. Two planes — *Reno's Raider* and *Wabbit Twacks*, flown by 1st Lt. James E. Foster — were hit by "continuously tracking flak about 40 seconds and one minute [respectively] before bombs away." Allison's aircraft "received a direct burst beneath the pilot's compartment, started into a steep spiral and crashed about 7

Final Missions

miles SW of Valognes, France." One chute was observed.

The men aboard *Reno's Raider* on May 8th were:

- Capt. Randolph G. E. Jacobs — Commander
- 2nd Lt. Earl T. Allison — Pilot
- 2nd Lt. John Q. Curtin — Navigator
- 2nd Lt. Jack C. Nagel — Bombardier
- Tech. Sgt. William F. Laubenstein — Radio Operator
- Staff Sgt. William A. Clements — Engineer/Top Turret
- Staff Sgt. Vernon H. Kaufman — Ball Turret Gunner
- 2nd Lt. Lester W. Hall— Tail Gunner
- Staff Sgt. Kenneth N. Hougard — Waist/Flex Gunner
- Staff Sgt. James H. Grimmett — Waist/Flex Gunner

Foster's B-17 was "hit by a burst between the tail and waist doors and went into a very steep uncontrollable dive; [it] was seen to hit the ground still burning, and the tail gunner seemed to be blown out, with no chutes observed; crashed near Le Foyer, France," according to MACR

Reno's Raider; Earl Allison's Crew's Final Fortress.
(Courtesy of 384thBombGroup.com)

number 4561. There were no survivors. The eleven men aboard Wabbit Twacks were:

- 1st Lt. James E. Foster — Pilot
- 2nd Lt. Clifford L. Johnson — Co-pilot
- 2nd Lt. Joseph K. Uniszkiewicz — Navigator
- Tech Sgt. Robert C. Corpening — Togglier
- Tech Sgt. Thomas W. Corbett — Radio Operator
- Tech Sgt. James D. Boone, Jr. — Engineer
- Staff Sgt. Jimmy L. Overcash, Jr. — Ball Turret Gunner
- Staff Sgt. Sigmund S. Matican — Tail Gunner
- Staff Sgt. John J. Stevens — Waist Gunner
- Staff Sgt. Thomas T. Cochran — Waist Gunner
- Major Russell A. Sanders — Observer

[There isn't much to be found on these brave and unfortunate men, other than references to the crash itself. But their names are remembered, by the people of Normandy, by those who study history and by those who read this book.]

In Earl Allison's aircraft, despite only one chute being seen by witnesses, five men managed to escape the plane with their lives. Navigator John Curtin, radio operator William F. Laubenstein, tail gunner Lester W. Hall, and waist gunners Kenneth N. Hougard and James H. Grimmett all survived the crash by parachuting to the ground safely. Unfortunately, pilot Earl Allison, co-pilot Randolph Jacobs, bombardier Jack C. Nagel, engineer William A. Clements and ball turret gunner Vernon H. Kaufman were not able to get out and perished in the crash.

Four of the five survivors — Quinn, Laubenstein, Hall and Grimmett were taken prisoner by the Germans and spent the remainder of the war in POW camps. Parts of their very interesting stories are related in Chapter Nine of this book. Kenneth Hougard managed to Evade and Escape the Germans, with help from ordinary French citizens and

Final Missions

the intrepid French Underground Resistance. His story is told word for word in Chapter Ten, written by his own hand upon his return to base at Grafton-Underwood. It is the stuff of Hollywood cinema and could very well be its own full-length book or movie.

Both planes — Allison's and Foster's — went down in almost the same location that Herb Small's plane had gone down just eleven days earlier, near Bricquebec and Rocheville in Normandy. In 1997, fifty-three years later, the two towns of Bricquebec and Rocheville built and dedicated a memorial to the crews of Herbert Small and James Foster to mark their deaths and sacrifice. It is a beautiful bronze statue of a heavily damaged B-17 with its left wing shot off, perched atop a granite pylon. It doesn't include the Earl Allison crew, which is surprising, considering how close to the same location they went down on that same May 8th mission as Foster. I have found no explanation for why Allison's crew was not included.

In May of 2023, my wife and I were able to visit that monument, as we were, by coincidence or fate, staying in a bed and breakfast outside of Ste-Mere-Eglise only a fifteen-minute drive away from its location. The B-17 Memorial is like so many of the monuments and memorials throughout the region; humble, dignified and respectful. The site includes the beautiful monument itself, a large plaque with the twenty-one names of the men lost in the two crews, and two signs with the details of the crashes written in French, English and German. The plaque reads, in English and French, "In memory of the crewmen of two American B-17s fallen near the towns of Bricquebec (le 08 Mai 1944) [and] Rocheville (le 27 Avril 1944).

> **[I find it very interesting, and possibly a testament to the character of the people of Normandy, that a German translation (accompanied on the sign by the German flag) is included in the memorial. I could offer thoughts on how that came to be, but I think I'll let readers make their own conclusions.]**

Jamaica Mary

Bombs Away

Seeing the memorial was an incredible addition to our trip, which included the visit to the American Cemetery in Normandy already related in the Introduction. We were also able to visit the site of the much-storied La Fiere Bridge battlefield to the west of Ste-Mere-Eglise, among many other notable and memorable locations. I mention the La Fiere Bridge because where we stayed was a bed and breakfast called The Old Farm of Amfreville, which played a part in the drama that unfolded in the Battle of La Fiere Bridge on and in the days that followed D-Day. In and of itself, the story is a fascinating chapter in the history of the 82nd Airborne Division, as one of the bloodiest battles in the war based on the size of the battlefield.

The war came to an abrupt and tragic end for Herbert W. Small on April 27th, 1944, and his departure was followed soon thereafter on May 8th by five of his closest brothers-in-arms. The men from his crew who survived the war — and all of their families — were then and are still now tasked with carrying on Herb's memory and that of the rest of the crew. By my efforts with this book, I am carrying the torch for a little while, both for my uncle and his crew and for the many other men mentioned here, however briefly. I hope to be able to add something substantial to the written memorial to the lives of these brave, patriotic and dedicated men, my uncle among them.

John R. McCrary wrote in *The First of the Many* "Damn it, somewhere a writer with the right words, an artist with the necessary keenness of perception must be found to capture the courage that is in these boys." I don't know if I am that writer with any kind of "keenness of perception," but I do know that I have a passion for telling this story… and hopefully that's enough.

Since I began studying the events of Herb Small's life and his death, I have become ever more fascinated by both the story of the 8th Air Force as a whole, the 384th Bomb Group specifically, and by Herb's (and the men he flew with) small part in that story. Along with the monument dedicated to him and the other men from the 384th in Normandy, there is a memorial back in his hometown of Sheffield, Massa-

Final Missions

Monument in Bricquebec, France to the crews of Herbert Small and James Foster. (Photo by the author.)

chusetts, made up of a stone monument and a line of trees planted in remembrance, one for each of the town's sons lost in World War II. I'm sure if I spent time looking for them, I'd find similar memorials dedicated to the other men he flew with, particularly for the ones who were from small towns like Sheffield, who seem to suffer these losses of their local heroes somehow more deeply than in larger cities.

Very few of us in modern times, outside of military veterans themselves, can even begin to imagine the kind of trauma and loss these men were subjected to on a regular basis during the war. Is it any wonder so many men came home from World War II with lifelong struggles with anger, depression and alcoholism? What we now know of as PTSD[Post Traumatic Stress Disorder] was not really understood eighty years ago. Men were considered "shell-shocked," "flak-happy" or "battle-fatigued," or some other term that made it seem less serious and damaging than it

Memorial to Herbert W. Small in Sheffield, Massachusetts.

Final Missions

really was. These men endured some of the worst conditions, away from everyone they knew and loved, for ideals that most now only recognize as bumper-sticker or campaign slogans. There is a reason they have been dubbed "the Greatest Generation." I've heard some people minimize that over the years…or even mock it. Ironically, those who mock them are only free to do so because of the sacrifice made by so few for the sake of so many, to borrow a bit of the spirit of the famous quote by Winston Churchill.

The obituary for Staff Sgt. Vernon H. Kaufman, shared with me in correspondence with his lovely sister Mrs. Donna Wiley, contained a beautiful prayer that I'd like to share here, as I feel it is an appropriate way to close this chapter:

> "My God, give such grace to the
> loved one that by faith they may
> say of this gallant son and brother:
> 'His sun went down in the morning,
> While all was fair and bright;
> But it shines today on the faraway hills,
> In the land that knows no night.'"

Bombs Away

Staff Sgt. Vernon H. Kaufman. (Courtesy of 384thBombGroup.com)

S/Sgt. Marion L. Parker. (Courtesy 384thBombGroup.com)

Lt. John M. Sewack (Courtesy 384thBombGroup.com)

Final Missions

B-17s of the 384th lined up after landing away at RAF Boxted.
(Courtesy of 384thBombGroup.com)

The Intelligence Office at Grafton-Underwood.

Bombs Away

Reverend Method Billy blesses the crew of We Dood It before a mission.
(Courtesy of Paul Teal and Sam Coleman.)

The Fortress that Herb Small went down in. B-17G #297136.
(Courtesy of 384thBombGroup.com)

POWs

9

"There were two barbed wire fences ten feet high surrounding the camp. Between the two fences was another fence of rolled wire about four feet high. Fifty feet inside the wire fences was a warning wire. Prisoners could be expected to be shot if they crossed the warning wire. Posted at close intervals were armed guard towers with search lights. Guards with dogs patrolled the perimeters."
    T/Sgt. William F. Laubenstein, *A Quiet Hero*.

During World War II, there were an estimated 124,079 U.S. Army personnel who were held as Prisoners of War (POWs) by our enemies. Of these, roughly 41,057 belonged to the Army Air Forces. Of that number, approximately 28,000 were members of the Eighth Air Force flying and fighting out of England over the European continent. There were also a staggering 26,000 airmen of the Eighth Air Force Killed in Action. Back at the bases in England, the men usually had no way of knowing for certain, regardless of how many parachutes were reported as being seen as an aircraft was on its way down, whether the men from those aircraft were dead or alive. They could not know if their friends and fellow airmen were POWs, if they had Evaded and Escaped behind enemy lines or if they had perished in the crash, except when they occasionally received word via letters, the Red Cross or the various Underground groups.

The 384th Bombardment Group out of Grafton-Underwood had a total of 428 men Killed in Action (KIA), 62 men listed as Missing in Action (MIA), 116 who evaded capture by the Germans and 878 Prisoners of War (POW). My great-uncle Herbert Small knew some in each category very well, as he was their colleague, crewmate or friend...or all three. There are too many stories in the 384th alone to tell in such a limited space to be able to do the stories justice. However, Chapter Ten is dedicated to the story of tail gunner Kenneth Hougard, whose story I will let speak for itself. It's an unbelievable read and a great example of the kind of incredible story so many of these men were part of. Keep in mind while reading it that the man was only twenty-one years old at the time, down behind enemy lines and being helped by people who would be killed if they were discovered to be aiding "the enemy."

Of the men that Herb flew with often and knew well, there were three that I know of that survived being shot down who became POWs in the German Stalag system; radio operator Staff Sgt. William F. Laubenstein, waist gunner Sgt. James H. Grimmett and navigator 1st Lt. Joseph L.G. Cittadini. Both Laubenstein and Cittadini wrote extensively about their POW experiences in their war memoirs, including some incredible detail about the prison camps, treatment by guards, overall conditions and other aspects of life as a POW.

The men were shot down on consecutive days; Cittadini over Germany on May 7th, 1944, followed by Grimmett and Laubenstein on May 8th over France. Cittadini's crew was able to crash-land, and all ten men onboard survived to become POWs. Their story, as told by Lt. Cittadini, is riveting, and some of it will be included in this chapter. Grimmett and Laubenstein were two of the five men who survived the shooting down of the Earl Allison crew *Reno's Raider* on May 8th, the

POWs

A member of the ground crew keeps watch for Forts that may never return. (Courtesy of Paul Teal and Sam Coleman)

other three survivors being John Q. Curtin, Lester W. Hall and Kenneth N. Hougard. John Curtin and Lester Hall also became POWs. They were sent to Stalag VIIA in Moosberg and Stalag III in Sagan-Silesia respectively. The five of them survived the crash by bailing out at 26,000 feet, a prospect almost as terrifying as perishing aboard a burning and doomed B-17.

Many of the POW stories contain similar elements regarding how the men came to be captured by the Germans. Often the flak crews who shot them down were able to relay their approximate crash locations to other German soldiers in the vicinity, or in the case of those who crashed in Germany, like Cittadini, to local citizens or "home guard" members, who were usually men too old or boys too young for military service. When men bailed out over an occupied country -- France, Holland or Belgium in particular -- they had a much better chance of evading capture because of helpful and resourceful locals and members of the Resistance aiding them, at great risk to their own lives. Bailing out over Germany meant the men would almost certainly be captured by the

Bombs Away

Germans and sent to the Stalags.

Since the Americans performed Precision Daytime Bombing, rather than bombing indiscriminately at night as the British did, they did not enjoy the advantage of the cover of darkness to aid in their hiding or escaping from the Germans. Often men in the same plane met very different fates, with one or two evading detection and escaping into the Resistance Underground while the rest succumbed to being captured. It was sometimes quite literally down to where the wind blew them.

[Interestingly, because of that distinction between the daylight bombing of the Americans and the nighttime bombing of the British, the German citizenry often had a generally better attitude toward the American airmen. In their eyes, the British didn't really care where the bombs wound up, as long as they hit Germany and Germans. Possibly the British thought that way as a retaliation for the many months they endured of the Germans bombing London and other British cities with the same indiscretion. The Americans, conversely, at least seemed to be trying to mainly hit true military and industrial targets. Until, of course, the focus turned to the blanket bombing of entire cities.]

A great example of how men could be scattered about when they bailed out comes from the crew of Earl Allison being shot down on May 8th over France. Laubenstein and Grimmett landed outside of the small village of St.-Jacques-de-Nehou, just to the south of where their plane crashed near Bricquebec-en-Cotentin. St.-Jacques-de-Nehou is roughly four miles west of Ste-Colombe, near the Douve River, where Kenneth Hougard would wind up taking refuge. They all bailed out at roughly 26,000 feet — nearly five miles up — so it's not surprising that they could come down so far apart. Hougard tells in his story about waiting to pull his ripcord until he was at around 2,000 feet of altitude, meaning that he was in free-fall for about four and a half miles at speeds well above 100 miles per hour.

Laubenstein and Grimmett were able to initially evade capture for about two and a half days by hiding out on a farm near St.-Jacques-de-Nehou, with help from members of the French Resistance. William Laubenstein described his capture in his unpublished memoir *A Quiet Hero*: "The French were warned to stay 'holed up' for two and a half days. They also found out that Grimmett was in the little village called St. Jacques and wanted to know if I wanted to meet up with him. I wanted to, so we crossed the fields at night to a farmer's house where I met Grimmett. Grimmett was in French clothes and was glad to see me because he didn't know if I had safely gotten out of the plane and made it to the ground. However, the next evening, while we were having dinner at the French man's house, we were captured. Apparently, there were other Frenchmen that were aware of us and reported our whereabouts to the nearby Germans. The Germans came into the house with drawn pistols and captured us. There was a black man in the house with us and he tried to escape across the field, but he didn't make it and was shot and killed."

Laubenstein and Grimmett were taken by car to a prison in St. Lo and then moved to another prison in Caen, each for only one day. In a surprising twist, a few days later, Laubenstein recalls "…while we were locked in an outdoor prison, Grimmett and I had a weird experience. At about 4-5 PM, an air raid took place and, wouldn't you know, broke open Grimmett's cell door but not mine. It stayed securely locked. Grimmett took off and left me there. On the following day, I was put into a German truck and headed out of Paris to Frankfurt, Germany. The ride took us through the Arc de Triumph in France — that was indeed a great memory — even in the hands of the Germans." The two were reunited eventually when Grimmett was once again captured and sent to Stalag Luft IV. Laubenstein's memoirs offer no explanation for why Grimmett took off and didn't try to free his buddy; perhaps there was no time, or maybe he panicked.

T/Sgt. Laubenstein reported about Stalag Luft IV that "we were

Bombs Away

treated properly but our living conditions were severe. There were an estimated 9,000 to 10,000 POWs in our camp. The officers were in one section and the enlisted men in another section. Our days were spent roaming the perimeter of the compound, reading, playing cards, and we had roll call twice each day."

Aboard B-17 *Goin Dog*, after losing two engines due to mechanical trouble on the bombing run to Berlin on May 7th, pilot Theodore Goller, Jr. and navigator Lt. Joseph Cittadini were forced to fall out of formation, and subsequently dropped their bombs at about 6,000 feet to lighten their plane's load and conserve fuel. Their hope was to fly out of Germany and limp home to England, but they knew they would be extremely vulnerable out of formation and with only two functioning engines. They were soon set upon by a pair German Messerschmitt Me-210 fighters and ducked into cloud cover in an attempt to evade. At this point, navigator Cittadini made an announcement to the crew:

"Navigator to crew…we're below 10,000 feet. We won't be able to climb to altitude on two engines so remove your oxygen masks and try to relax. We're in the Bremen area of Germany. If we are forced to bail out for any reason it is a good long walk to Luxembourg which is roughly southwest of this position. Beyond that is France and the Maginot Line which is occupied by the Germans. If you head directly east, you will come into the Netherlands. I have no information on whether they have an underground to assist Allied airmen."

> **[This communication from Cittadini to the crew, as he was forced to consider the possibility of being shot down and captured, is striking to me. There's something so matter of fact and almost casual in the way I read him saying those words -- it speaks to the character, professionalism and maturity of him and his crew. Cittadini was actually twenty-seven years old at the time and would have been considered one of the "old men" by many of the younger airmen.]**

POWs

They continued to be harassed by flak while losing power and altitude and were eventually left no choice but to attempt a crash landing. All the while, the gunners continued to fire upon ground targets when they presented themselves, showing their fighting spirit until the very end. Upon scrambling out of the downed B-17, they were quickly met by German soldiers and, as they were unarmed and deep in enemy territory, they had no other option than to surrender.

Cittadini's crew on May 7th:

- 2nd Lt. Theodore Goller, Jr. – Pilot
- 2nd Lt. Gregory L. Martin – Co-pilot
- 2nd Lt. Joseph L.G. Cittadini – Navigator
- Flight Officer Eugene P. Grilli – Bombardier
- S/Sgt. Irvin L. Bier – Radio Operator
- S/Sgt. Clarence E. Reed – Engineer/Top Turret
- S/Sgt. Walter E. Wearne – Ball Turret Gunner
- Sgt. Horace M. Walton – Tail Gunner
- Sgt. Arthur H. Way – Waist Gunner
- Sgt. Roy F. Howell – Waist Gunner

Cittadini's group of ten was rounded up neatly by a German soldier who had witnessed the crash, and as none of the airmen were carrying weapons and a few were wounded, the Americans did not put up a fight. They were marched through the countryside over the course of a couple of days and kept in very cold and bleak living conditions. Then they were transported by truck and finally by rail to the Dulag Luft, which was a three-part system for processing Prisoners of War. It consisted of an interrogation center, a hospital and a transit camp that was the final stop before men were sent to one of the dozens of Stalag Lufts, the German Prisoner of War camps, that were scattered throughout Germany and Poland mostly.

To the Germans' credit, the wounded men were given medical

Bombs Away

Theodore Goller Crew: Back L-R: Clarence E. Reed T.; Roy F. Howell; Irwin L. Bier; Arthur H. Way; Horace M. Wallton; Samuel V. Houston;   Front L--R: Theodore Goller, Jr.; James E. Geary; Joseph L.G. Cittadini; James J. "Jeff" Brown.
(Courtesy of 384thBombGroup.com)

Joseph Cittadini is captured, along with the rest of the Ted Goller crew. I believe Cittadini is the man on the far left helping his crewmate.
(Courtesy of 384thBombGroup.com)

POWs

attention and at least a small amount of food, and Cittadini recalled relatively decent treatment overall during their initial phase of captivity.

The stories of German treatment of POWs vary greatly, from relatively mild and even compassionate, to cruel and sadistic, and many variations in between. Some of that difference depended upon whom had done the capturing...rank and file Wehrmacht soldiers or the villainous S.S. The average German soldiers were often not much different in many regards than our own G.I.s; they were professional soldiers or conscripts, fighting for their country and trying to stay alive, usually believing in what they were fighting for. But many weren't true Nazis, unlike the S.S.

There are many instances in the stories of the POWs that have a common element, which is very interesting. Sometimes, when American officers made an authoritative and logical appeal for better conditions of some kind, the German soldiers would capitulate. Cittadini writes of one such exchange between himself — an American Lieutenant — and a German of the same rank, regarding the very poor living conditions his crew was being subjected to in the first days of captivity. The German officer was angry because the B-17 crew had fired upon his flak tower as they were going down and killed two Germans and wounded a third. The soldier was rightfully upset. Cittadini responded, "When we were flying, we were at war with each other. You were shooting at us, and we were returning the fire. You were our enemy then. Now we are your prisoners and demand that we be afforded treatment in accordance with agreements reached by the International Convention at Geneva, Switzerland for prisoners of war."

The American's story continues: "The German officer gave it a moment of thought. He turned to the guard, gave him some orders and left without further word to us." Not long after that encounter, the wounded men received medical attention and some small improvements in their conditions. It was a small victory, but even the smallest of victories could mean the difference between life and death, especially where medical attention was concerned. It seems that the German soldiers, being as well-trained and disciplined as they were, responded well to appeals from authority, even when that authority was the captured enemy.

There were many occasions where critically wounded men aboard a B-17 who would not have survived the long return trip to England were reluctantly bailed out by their crew. The hope was, however desperate, that the wounded men would be captured by the Germans in time to receive life-saving medical attention. Many an airman who might have been lost was saved by the compassion of the Germans on the ground, enemies or not, speaking once again to some element of common decency and humanity, even among a mortal enemy.

Cittadini's trip took him through Frankfurt then by train to Stalag Luft III. He wrote in his memoir *20th Mission*: "During the journey, which was a pleasant ride, we discussed the fantasy of effecting an escape to try to make our way back to France. The train brought us to Sagan [Germany] the next morning." His experience differs greatly from that of Laubenstein, who reported that he was transported by rail in a very crowded cattle car to Stalag Luft IV, which was nearly to the border of Poland. There was a large difference in the treatment of officers versus the treatment of enlisted men by the Germans, with the former getting the much better deal in many regards. That may very well explain much of the difference in these two men's experiences.

Unfortunately, not all POWs reported their travel to the Stalags as being a pleasant journey by rail. After a quick shower, T/Sgt. Laubenstein was herded into a cattle car, the infamous "Forty and Eights," ("40 hommes — 8 chevaux" was printed in French on the side) named for their ability to transport forty men or eight horses, but often packed with sixty to seventy POWs. Stories of men captured during the Battle of the Bulge reported being kept in the overcrowded rail cars for multiple days with no food, little water and nowhere to relieve themselves other than a designated corner of the boxcar.

William Laubenstein recalled the conditions in Stalag Luft IV, near Stettin, Germany, almost on the border of Poland: "Stalag life was a very bad experience. The Germans couldn't feed us properly because they didn't have enough food for so many of us. In the morning after

POWs

An unidentified POW camp with American prisoners.
(Courtesy of 384thBombGroup.com)

roll call, we were locked up in our barracks, brought our coffee and hard stale bread. At noon, we were lucky to get soup, usually watery, with a few pieces of cabbage. For the evening meal we were given a couple of boiled potatoes and that was it." The men were on a starvation diet that provided them far fewer calories (and far fewer vitamins, minerals and grams of protein) than were needed to truly sustain human life. They were very slowly wasting away.

"It wasn't until August or September of 1944 that we were saved by the American Red Cross food parcels. The parcels contained sugar cubes, powdered milk, cigarettes, soap, Spam, prunes and a few other items. These parcels were also supplemented by packages sent by our wives and family members. I went into camp weighing about 155 lbs. and weighed about 95 lbs. when we were liberated on May 3rd [1945]."

An unidentified POW camp with American prisoners.
(Courtesy of 384thBombGroup.com)

He lost more than a third of his body weight over the course of roughly one year in captivity.

The men at Stalag Luft IV, according to Laubenstein's memoirs, were not required to work, but life was nonetheless very difficult, with malnutrition, dysentery, scurvy — caused by severe vitamin deficiency — and common pests like lice being a constant source of distress and torment. Laubenstein's writing provides incredibly vivid detail on life at Stalag Luft IV, including the layout of the camp, the types of prisoners contained in each section, the quality and quantity of food, medical treatment and countless other details. There are many such stories of American POWs taking great care to study the details of how the camps were set up and how they functioned. Their motivation could have been that they were seeking ways to attempt an escape, that they were making a mental record as a way of documenting their mistreatment or it

POWs

could have been simply to keep their minds occupied at a time when they suffered from extreme boredom. Whatever the reason, their collective memories have helped to build a detailed record of how POWs were treated by the Germans in World War II.

Joseph Cittadini's memoirs also give some remarkable detail of life at Stalag Luft III, in Sagan, Germany, cataloguing the various items that were issued to each man upon arrival, such as "an eating bowl, cup, knife, fork and spoon…two lightweight German issue blankets and one U.S. Army blanket…[plus]…a large burlap sack which we filled with excelsior [tiny strips of wood shavings]…that was to be our mattress." The POWs referred to themselves as "Kriegies," which was short for the German word Kriegsgefangene (Prisoners of War) and spent much of their time in the camps devising ingenious and innovative solutions to the myriad problems they encountered on a daily basis, one of the biggest of which was simple boredom.

Onother problem that the men in Stalag Luft III overcame was a serious shortage of equipment for cooking and baking, because they were responsible for preparing their own meals. The few pots and pans that were provided fell very short of what was needed to make even rudimentary meals for the men. Cittadini recalled of the efforts made by another prisoner; "In a week or two by saving the empty cans from dried milk and margarine cans by rummaging in the 'tin can dump,' enough cans were at hand to make pans for baking. His tools were a wooden mallet of rough pine which he made himself, a dinner knife, and a stool whose seat was made of two boards with a slight space between them. By hammering a nail in the stool at one end between the cracks he achieves an efficient cutting tool. The dinner knife placed in the crack, using the nail as the fulcrum, is used to cut the sheet metal. The cut pieces are seamed together to make a sheet large enough for the pan size he was making. By folding the sides up and the corners in we have a serviceable pan for baking."

Since radio broadcasts from outside of Germany were forbidden — the only news was from German Radio Broadcasts, which was mostly propaganda telling of German victories — POWs showed their ingenuity by building radios from various parts scrounged from sources around the camp. And since the possession of a radio by prisoners was also forbidden, the men would form small "radio groups," with each of six or seven men holding a different part of the radio, which was only assembled when they came together to listen to outside broadcasts, like the BBC. Cittadini describes these actions by saying, "Underground secretive operations were always in progress. We had the radio group each holding a part of the radio. At the prearranged time, members of this group would convene at an assembly point to put the parts together and tune in the BBC."

These small acts of rebellion by the prisoners, either to help make their daily living conditions a little more tolerable or to gain some information and intelligence from the outside world, were critical to keeping

Liberation of the POW camp Stalag Luft VII-A outside of Moosberg, Germany. (Courtesy of 384thBombGroup.com).

POWs

their minds and bodies engaged and their morale up. The men considered these actions their small way of keeping the war against Germany going and never fully surrendering, even though they were in the prison camp. Such collective acts of defiance were likely part of the inspiration for the hit television comedy Hogan's Heroes, two decades later.

> **[One passage from Joseph Cittadini struck me as odd and interesting all at once, in his description of the living conditions for officers at the Stalag: "All told, the conditions could be described as livable. Our accommodations back at Grafton-Underwood, England were not any better except there we did have fuel for our stove at our air base. We were happy and could not expect more than what we received." I can't tell if that speaks well of the conditions at the Stalag or poorly of the conditions at Grafton-Underwood. Or perhaps it is simply part of the normal tendency of people over time to soften their memories of a very difficult time, coming to believe things were not as bad as they really were at the time. His memoirs were written many decades after the war.]**

In late winter and spring of 1945, the war was not going well for the Germans. They had tried and failed with their last-ditch effort to turn the tide with the massive counter-offensive and breakout that became known as the Battle of the Bulge, one of the largest and most famous battles in military history. Germany's enemies were closing in -- the Russian Red Army from the east and the Americans and Brits from the west. Hitler's time was running out, and he knew it. The Stalag prison system was spread wide throughout Germany and into occupied Austria, Czechoslovakia, Poland and East Prussia. As the enemies of the Third Reich drew nearer, the Stalags needed to be emptied of their prisoners, and transportation was very difficult to come by. That meant that many of the prisoners had to walk.

Bombs Away

Many of the American POW's stories culminated in a very long, very cold, very deadly forced march, fleeing the invading forces from east or west, heading deeper into the interior of the German "Fatherland." Men who were already severely undernourished, exhausted, battling dysentery and all manner of other diseases and discomfort were forced to march on foot for hours through the bitterly cold German winter, which was one of the coldest on record at the time. The temperature often plummeted to twenty and even forty degrees below zero. Many good soldiers and airmen who may have otherwise survived the war and made it home to their loved ones perished in this futile and foolish maneuver by the Germans.

William Laubenstein describes his experience; "Late in January 1945, Stalag Luft IV airmen could see a distant flash of artillery fire, which meant the Russian army was not far away. Some of the sick and wounded prisoners were evacuated and put on a train. On February 6th, the remaining POWs were sent out on foot. An estimated number of about 6,000 men were told the march would last only three days. However, this march, known as the Death March, lasted for eighty-six days and we walked 600 miles during one of the cruelest winters on record." It's hard to believe that any man could have survived this ordeal, and it is a testament to the toughness and unrelenting determination of these men to have been able to survive.

In February of 1945, Cittadini's group of POWs was marched, pulled by horse-drawn cart and finally loaded into the infamous Forty & Eights for the trip from Sagan to Nürnburg (Nuremberg), where they were put into another camp, Stalag Luft XIII-D. They remained there until early April, when they were informed that General Patton's Third Army was within fifty-five miles of the camp and that they must be prepared to move out again immediately. Thankfully, the weather conditions were much better than during the January and February marches, but the food situation was no better. They finally made it to Stalag Luft VII-A outside of Moosberg, Germany, where they spent the last two weeks of the war.

POWs

Cittadini gives a great description of the camp's liberation by General Patton: "Sunday, April 29 brought the General George Smith Patton's Third Army into the outskirts of Moosberg. Machine guns chattered from time to time. An occasional rifle was fired. Perhaps it was the Moosberg home guard putting up a brave last stand. Early after noon, the firing ceased. General Patton came into the camp. Somehow, I was able to squeeze into the room to listen to him tell us that we were great soldiers and would soon be transported to France. His single pearl handle pistol hung jauntily from his hip. We had heard that the other pistol was given to Dinah Shore."

It was General Patton's firm belief that the creativity, ingenuity and adaptability of the American fighting man was a critical factor in our victory. In an interview with a lieutenant who had served with Patton, related by Frank Sisson, who had also served under Patton, in his book *I Marched with Patton: A Firsthand Account of World War II Alongside one of the U.S. Army's Greatest Generals*, this point is confirmed. "'I heard General Patton speak once,' the lieutenant said." Patton said one of the keys to our victory was "'strong, patriotic men.

POWs liberated at Moosberg, Germany. (Courtesy of 384thBombGroup.com)

Bombs Away

The crew of *April's Fool*, crashed in Hamburg, Germany area, July 25, 1943, and spent the remainder of the war as POWs. L-R Standing: R.O. Henley, Jr.; Warren B. Dillon; Ralph J. Hall; Rodney W. House; L-R squatting: Homer J. Cocklin; Paul E. McNeal; Reamond C. Smiley; Smith J. Davis; Albert R. Valcour (Courtesy of Mikayla Leech.)

April's Fool. (Courtesy of Mikayla Leech.)

POWs

The 'dogface' GI Joe types that are mentally clever and physically strong. On the other hand, the German soldiers came from a different world. They were certainly obedient enough, but they were rigid and lacked the ingenuity that was natural for our guys. When it came to trading blows with the enemy, we came out on top because we were more innovative.'" Sisson goes on to tell of Patton's other reasons, but his main point was that innovative and creative spirit of the men.

    Some of the Eighth Air Force men spent just a few weeks or months as POWs, while others spent as much or even more time in the Stalags as they had at their various bases in England flying missions. Each man's experience, it seems, was somehow similar but also unique in certain ways, and for the most part, these men kept up their fighting spirit, bonded deeply with their fellow prisoners and helped each other as much as possible to survive a very difficult experience. Some have commented in their stories that they were glad they weren't held captive by the Japanese on the Pacific front, as the Japanese were known for their sadistic brutality and inhumane treatment of Prisoners of War.

    Lt. Col. Joseph Cittadini's *20th Mission, a short account as well as my memory serves*, begins with an interesting story of an encounter he had much later in life on a routine trip to a doctor's office. I thought it a fitting way to end this chapter. When I can, I prefer to let these men speak for themselves, rather than giving you my thoughts. Cittadini wrote:

    "I am in my 80th year and in relatively good health. I am a retired Air Force Reserve Lt. Colonel with 19 successful missions.... I want to tell you a little bit about my 20th. Before I do, let me add an anecdote. Perhaps it will provide food for thought to counteract some of the stories you've heard about the abusive nature of the German soldiers: Recently I escorted a friend to a doctor's office. While we were waiting, my friend asked me about the treatment we received in Stalag Luft III. He asked me if we were subjected to hurtful treatment. I told him that my association with the German Military personnel was about as good as we could expect. We did have many months of close to a starvation diet.

Bombs Away

At times we were subjected to harsh conditions due to weather. No time did I suffer personal abuse and in retrospect I must say that they tried to conform to the requirements of the Geneva Convention of 1929 regarding treatment of POWs. They didn't have much to give us as POWs, but I feel sure that their depot troops and civilians did not fare as well as we did because, in addition to the supplies they afforded us, we received Red Cross food.

The waiting room was small. What we said was easily heard by all present. A man and his wife sitting in the corner were listening intently. When there was a pause in our conversation the man spoke up and asked me which POW camp I had been in. As we talked, we found that we were on the same march from Nürnberg to Moosburg and that General Patton's Third Army liberated us. He then told us a bit about his capture. His right arm had been badly mangled getting free from his parachute after his plane was destroyed by flak. The Germans brought him to a large hospital nearby. The doctor who attended him told him that the damage to his arm was so bad it had to be removed. The next day the surgeon who was to operate asked the wounded pilot if he would submit to an innovative, unprecedented operation that might save his arm. The surgeon cautioned the patient that if he could save the arm, he mustn't expect it to be of much use. Our friend waiting here in the doctor's office with us said, 'Whatever the outcome of the operation it couldn't be any worse than losing the arm to amputation.' At this point he got up from his chair, lifted his right arm, flexed his muscle and proudly exclaimed, 'He sure did a great job!' After the war he learned that the German doctor who had operated was a world-renowned neurosurgeon."

Evade and Escape

10

We were up at about 26,000 feet, and I remembered you were to delay your jump if this sort of thing happened to you. So I went down a long way before I pulled the ripcord. I must have been at about 2,000 feet when I did. A funny thing happened then. The chute wouldn't open out and I had to pull it out with my hands. - S/Sgt. Kenneth Hougard.
- Escape and Evade Report EE-829.

Staff Sergeant Kenneth N. Hougard was a tail gunner and waist gunner who was assigned to the 384th Bombardment Group (Heavy), 544th Bombardment Squadron (Heavy) on the same day as Lieutenant Herbert W. Small; November 5, 1943. Hougard flew twenty-one missions with Herb. They flew a couple of other missions with other crews occasionally but were mostly on the same missions throughout their service together. Herb Small flew a total of twenty-seven missions — four of which did not earn Combat Mission Credit due to having to abort for weather or mechanical issues — so having Kenneth Hougard on twenty-one of those missions would make it safe to say that they knew each other pretty well.

I don't know the level of friendship they may have had, or if they had any relationship outside of a professional military association, but I know that at least one story about S/Sgt. Hougard warrants telling, which is why I am including it in this book about my uncle. Hougard's story is of his survival after being shot down when his Flying Fortress was hit by flak on his twenty-sixth official mission, bailing out and parachuting into German-occupied France.

Airmen were originally to be sent home when they achieved Combat Mission Credit for twenty-five missions. Kenneth Hougard was flying another mission, his twenty-sixth, because of the change in policy in early 1944 that upped the total mission requirement number to thirty. Any of the men who had achieved the twenty-five-mission mark at that point had to wonder how much longer their luck would hold out.

Picture from a newspaper clipping from an article featuring Kenneth Hougard's Evade and Escape story. (Courtesy of Laubenstein Family.)

Evade and Escape

[It is very plausible to say that the decision to increase the mission requirement to thirty probably cost a lot of good men their lives.]

The goal of the mission for May 8th was to eliminate another V-Weapon service bunker that was under construction in Sottevast, France. V-Weapons (Vergeltungswaffen, or Retaliation/ Vengeance Weapons) were one of Hitler's last-ditch weapons, designed to wreak fear and havoc mainly on the populace of London and other large British cities. They were long-range rockets that could be launched from as far as two hundred miles away and travel at speeds up to 400 miles per hour. Even late in the war, they were still a force to be reckoned with.

S/Sgt. Hougard was assigned as a waist gunner on this mission and with him were most of the regular guys from the crew of Earl Allison. All but one of the crew -- tail gunner 2nd Lt. Lester W. Hall-- had flown with Allison on previous missions. There was no reason to expect the mission would be any more difficult than any other they had been on.

The roster for the day was:

- Capt. Randolph G. E. Jacobs — Commander
- 2nd Lt. Earl T. Allison — Pilot
- 2nd Lt. John Q. Curtin — Navigator
- 2nd Lt. Jack C. Nagel — Bombardier
- T/Sgt. William F. Laubenstein — Radio Op.
- S/Sgt. William A. Clements — Engineer/Top Turret
- S/Sgt. Vernon H. Kaufman — Ball Turret Gunner
- 2nd Lt. Lester W. Hall— Tail Gunner
- S/Sgt. Kenneth N. Hougard — Waist Gunner
- SSgt. James H. Grimmett — Waist Gunner

Bombs Away

Kenneth Hougard featured in *Review*. (Courtesy of Laubenstein Family.)

They flew in a B-17G named *Reno's Raider* as the Group Lead. According to Sortie Report #2397, they were "hit by continuously tracking flak about 40 seconds before bomb release; [the] aircraft received [a] direct burst beneath the pilot's compartment; started into a deep spiral; crashed about 7 miles SW of Valognes, France."

Five crewmembers did not survive and were listed as Killed in Action on this mission: Randolph Jacobs, Earl Allison, Jack Nagel, Wil-

Evade and Escape

liam Clements and Vernon Kaufman. It was only the third mission since December 13th that they didn't fly with the team of Earl Allison as their pilot and Herbert Small as their co-pilot. I don't know if that is significant or not, but it seems noteworthy. Allison, Nagel, Laubenstein, Clements, Hougard and Grimmett had all flown more than twenty missions together with Herbert Small.

Did particular crews get to know each other — their skills, their tendencies, their strengths — well enough to become a literal well-oiled machine and perform better than newer crews? I would hazard a guess that they did, like any other team in sports, music or the military. Did missing a key component or two of a crew make a big difference...or enough of a difference to increase the odds of being shot down? I don't know the answers to those questions, but in this instance, some of the usual guys were not at their usual stations, and they were shot down.

Four of the surviving five men were captured by German forces and became Prisoners of War (POWs) for the remainder of the war; one of the five survivors — waist gunner Kenneth N. Hougard — was able to evade the Germans and escape without ever becoming a POW. Below is his story, the unedited version (except for correcting minor punctuation errors and typos) in his own words as his first submission in the Escape and Evasion Report, before military censors made some edits and redactions to it.

The story conveys a real sense of what it must have been like being behind enemy lines and being hidden by the people we were fighting to liberate. The French citizens who aided Hougard, whether they were actually part of the official Resistance or just kind people showing compassion, faced the very real threat of being arrested by the Germans and either shipped out to a concentration camp or executed on the spot. Hougard faced the challenge of the language barrier and encountered situations where luck or Providence alone seemed to save the day. The stress and strain of nearly two months in hiding under extreme circumstances comes through very clearly in his words.

Bombs Away

I present the story in its original form:

> Our target, I think, was gun emplacements in the Cherbourg area. We were just getting on the bomb run — bomb-bay doors were just opening, I remember — when we were hit in the mid-section with flak. I think it was 88mm. We started losing altitude quickly, and the interphone system was just dead. I didn't get any orders to bail out, but the waist gunner smelled powder and released the escape hatch, and I kicked open the escape hatch and bailed out.
>
> We were up at about 26,000 feet, and I remembered you were to delay your jump if this sort of thing happened to you. So I went down a long way before I pulled the ripcord. I must have been at about 2,000 feet when I did. A funny thing happened then. The chute wouldn't open out and I had to pull it out with my hands. When I was going down, I could hear bullets popping all round me. I looked below and saw one chute hit the ground before I did. There were three more chutes coming down above me — way up high. I don't know whether they came from my plane.
>
> [There are very practical reasons for waiting to pull the ripcord. First, there are numerous reports of some German pilots targeting men in their parachutes as they floated to the ground. And two, at 26,000 feet, a man under a deployed parachute would drop much more slowly and be at a high risk of passing out due to lack of oxygen.]
>
> I hit the ground in a field near Ste. Colombe, [pinpoints landing at 195988]. As soon as I got my feet on the ground, I ran over to a hedge at one side of the field and buried my parachute and Mae West [life preserver]. As I was hiding that chute, I counted 25 bullet holes in it. I realized then that the Germans must have been shooting at me as I came down, and that accounted for all those popping noises I heard while still up in the air.

Evade and Escape

I looked around for a good place to hide and finally chose a tree. I climbed up on the branches and stayed there until it got dark. From where I was sitting in the tree, I could see the tail end of a ship from my Squadron. It had a big "P" on it, and the last two numbers were "11." The last two numbers on my ship were "11," so it might have been mine. I could see another wrecked ship in the field, too, but I couldn't identify it.

When it got dark, I came out of the tree and found a barn in the field. It was moonlight, so I took it mighty easy going over to the barn. I could hear German motorcycle patrols on the road. I ate the candy from my escape kit and slept in the barn that night, burrowing in the hay.

The next day I watched from the barn and saw some German officers go to the one wrecked plane with the "P" on the tail. They took the radio equipment out and back to their car and then drove off. German soldiers kept wandering along and taking bits of the plane for souvenirs.

That same day some German soldiers came out to the plane and took three bodies from it. They put the bodies in boxes and started digging some graves. But then a German officer came along and said something to them. They quit digging, put the bodies into a truck and drove off.

I stayed in the barn all day waiting for night. As soon as it got dark, I went up to the house on the same farm and knocked at the door. Someone said something that sounded like "Come in," so I just walked in the door. There were two men and two women in the house. I told them I was an American aviator, but they apparently didn't understand or were afraid. All they would say is "No, no." I figured they didn't want to bother with me, so I left the farmhouse and started down a road to the south. I thought I was somewhere in the coastal defense area, and I knew it wasn't healthy to stay there. I wanted to get farther inland.

I kept going down the road, dodging those Nazi motorcycle patrols, until I hit a junction and a main highway. I went on down

Bombs Away

the highway where I came to a mill on the Douve River. From the mill I watched the bridge across the river for a good long while to make sure that I wouldn't run into any sentries. When I was certain no sentries were on the bridge, I crossed the river and made my way to Ste. Colombe.

I didn't want to walk right into Ste. Colombe, so I stopped at the first barn I came to just out of town. I slept there that night up in the hay. I guess I must have made some noise up there, because I heard someone putting a ladder up to the side of the barn. I jumped away from the side of the barn where I heard it and went to the other end of the haymow and tried to hide. But I could hear someone moving the ladder around to the window on the end of the barn I had gone to. I knew then I couldn't get away, so I just waited.

I heard the ladder being placed, and then a farmer came up into the haymow followed by his son. I told them, as best I could, that I was an American airman. They were both happy as heck, then, and brought the whole family up to see me. Someone was sent down to get me something to eat and came back with eggs, bread and cider.

Before the day was over it seemed like all the Frenchmen in the neighborhood knew I was there, and they were all bringing me odd bits of civilian clothes. Someone brought an old black coat, a beret, some black shoes that were too tight for me, and a pair of old coveralls. The farmer had a daughter about 19 years old who could speak a little English, and that helped to make myself understood. I asked her to get me someone who could speak English. She told me someone would come, so I waited in the barn. One Frenchmen came to see me and tried to give me some French money he had been given by another American airman who had been shot down.

That afternoon another Frenchman came who could speak good English. From that point on my journey was arranged.

The English-speaking Frenchman who came to see me on May 10 told me he was in a secret organization. I don't know what his name was and can't remember just what he looked like. Because there were so many Germans in the area around Ste. Colombe, he said he would send me to Paris. He made arrangements to have the farmer's daughter buy me a ticket the next morning. But later he met another Frenchman in another secret organization who advised him against sending me to Paris. He was told that there were 600 or more American airmen in Paris at that time and that it was becoming difficult to supply them with food.

Before this interpreter left, however, he made arrangements for me to leave the farmhouse the night of May 10. In the morning, a Frenchman with gray hair, heavily built, and about five feet 10 inches tall came with two bicycles. He and I then started for Rauville-la-Place (214948). When we arrived he took me to the home of Monsieur and Madam Picot Gaston, at Rauville-la-Place, par Ste.-Sauveur-le-Vicomte (Manche), where it was arranged that I stay.

I stayed with them for about a week and a half, sleeping in a room downstairs with a small French boy whose father was a prisoner of war. Most of the time I stayed in the house. Whenever Germans came, I hid in one of the rooms.

Gaston had a radio set, and I heard the news regularly. One day a French policeman from Cherbourg came to see Gaston. I thought that I was done for when I saw him walk in with his uniform and carrying arms. But he seemed to be in the secret organization as well. He had a radio set with him and left it with Gaston. While he was there, he took my name and serial number and told me that he would let Paris know about my being safe and that Paris would let London know.

Monsieur Gaston seemed to know a lot about the underground. He knew names of a lot of people in secret organizations. He had hidden another American who he called "Mississippi," and had sent him to a farm near Denneville.

A second interpreter came to see me one day and brought me some books to read. He had been a prisoner of war in Germany and was now hiding some Belgians from the Germans.

While at Rauville-la-Place another Frenchman came to see me from Ste.-Sauveur-le-Vicomte who was called Monsieur Octave (phonetic spelling). This man was finding hiding places for me. He was a short fellow, with a black mustache, and he always wore a big stiff, white collar. Every time I saw him he was well dressed, and always came on a bicycle. He used to come to bring me news and on one occasion brought me some handkerchiefs.

My helpers heard that the Germans were going to put a gun in a field near Gaston's place; so it was decided that I be moved to a safer place. Monsieur Octave had found a farm for me where it would be quiet and less dangerous.

Gaston and I left on an afternoon (I don't remember the date) in Gaston's horse-drawn buggy. Monsieur Octave went ahead on a bicycle to guide us. First, we went to Ste.-Sauveur-le-Vicomte and then to a large farm just out of Ste.-Sauveur-de-Pierre-Pont (147890). When we arrived at the farm, I was introduced to an old man there whose name I can't remember. There were about 15 people on the farm. I remember a girl about 20 whose name was Marie Rose, and two brothers whose names were Auguste and Ernest.

At this farm the second interpreter, who worked at some place in Cherbourg, came to see me to bring me some books. Monsieur Gaston, too, came to see me several times.

A priest, L'Abbe Raymond Hedouin, cure de St.-Nicholas-de-Pierrepont, came to visit me. He seemed to like me immediately and treated me wonderfully. He brought me shoes to replace those I had — which were much too tight. He also gave me new trousers and a sweater.

The Germans started putting some poles in the fields on the farm, so I was afraid I'd be found. When the interpreter from Cherbourg came to see me again, I told him I would like to move because there were too many people at the farm, and I thought it dangerous.

The third time L'Abbe Hedouin came to see me, he told me

to stay with him. He arranged that I borrow Marie Rose's bicycle, and I went along with him to his house. I think that was about May 23. We went to his house in St.-Nicholas-de-Pierrepont, and I stayed there that night.

The next day the interpreter from Cherbourg came to see me again. He told me that it was much safer for me to stay with the priest, and I was not to go back to the farm. L'Abbe Hedouin then went to the farm and told the people there that I had been sent away. I kidded him about fibbing to the people. But he said, "When a lie is for the good, it is all right."

L'Abbe Hedouin told everyone I was Belgian and was a nephew of his. He had only his maid with him, so I didn't have to worry much about being discovered. But I had to hide once in a while when Germans came to his house to get medical treatment. He used to help any of the Germans who needed medical care. Apparently, the word had got around among the Germans that he was such a kind man, for when one of them was hurt, he'd be brought to L'Abbe's house. L'Abbe used to tell me that he didn't like the Germans, but that individually they needed help sometimes just like any other people.

Gaston, the interpreter from Cherbourg, and Monsieur Octave used to all come to see me while I was staying at L'Abbe's house. They'd bring me news about what our bombers were doing and what was happening on the Russian front.

On June 5 Monsieur Octave came to see L'Abbe and brought him an armband with the Free French cross on it. He said the priest should wear the armband after the invasion, and then if he were captured by the Germans, he'd be treated as prisoner of war.

The day after the invasion, L'Abbe went to Ste.-Sauveur-de-Pierre-Pont to give services for a P-47 pilot who had crashed there. L'Abbe had the pilot's name and serial number when he returned, and also a picture he had taken from his body. I never did find out the name of the pilot.

Gaston came to see me again after that and took my picture

in order to make identification papers. He had the papers with him when he took my picture. He said he was also going to take a picture of the American he called "Mississippi."

We heard that the Germans were moving onto a hill just east of St. Nicholas. On June 10, L'Abbe, his maid, and I left and went to a farm about a mile to the west (143880) where we lived in a stable, sleeping in the hay. We were there when the Americans captured Ste.-Sauveur-le-Vicomte. Monsieur Octave got through the lines somehow and came to see us at the stable. He was very happy and told us that the Americans had taken the town.

Then the Germans began putting in positions near the farm, and a lot of German troops were coming by on their way to Baudreville. We began thinking about moving again.

One morning I wandered out to look at the railroad tracks the Americans had been bombing and walked right into a German officer and a German soldier. The officer asked me in French how many kilometers it was to Ste.- Sauveur-le-Vicomte. I told him as best I could in the poor French I had been able to pick up. He looked at me curiously, and then went on. I was terribly afraid that I would be caught for certain that time.

One morning the priest was told to move because too many Germans were in the neighborhood. The three of us packed our things in a wheelbarrow and went to another farm at la Hurie (143867). There were a lot of French people there who had evacuated from the areas where the fighting was going on. We all slept in the barn and ate our meals in the farmhouse.

I stayed at la Hurie for about three days, until the Germans started moving in there, too. L'Abbe and the French people there were starting to evacuate again. I told the priest that I was going to stay and wait for our lines to come up to me. L'Abbe was very worried about me, and afraid I would be hurt in the battle.

When I was at the farm just west of St. Nicholas, I had been told about two American officers who were hiding out at a farm at la Detrouse (143862). I had gone to see them twice, and L'Abbe had gone to give one of them, an infantry officer, treatment for grenade wounds. So I decided I'd now hide out with them.

When I left L'Abbe for the farm at la Detrousse, he and his maid were evacuating to LaHaye du Puits.

Some American evaders in Paris are being betrayed by girlfriends, according to the interpreter from Paris. He said that some of the Americans have several girlfriends and are betrayed to the Germans by one who becomes jealous.

The interpreter told me that an airman, Lt. Lawrence Hall, had been captured by the Germans. This may have been the lieutenant that went with us on the mission, acting as tail gunner.

> [Note: This turned out to not be the case. The tail gunner's name on this mission, according to Sortie Report #2397, was Lester W. Hall, not Lawrence Hall. However, there was a Lawrence M. Hall who had previously flown two missions as a waist gunner with the Herb Small and Kenneth Hougard crew, so perhaps he was just confusing the two similar names With both being waist gunners, they would have spent hours in the air together, side by side.]

On 1 July the Frenchmen who had helped me were ordered to evacuate by the Germans. I left them and joined two American officers who had been captured by the Germans, had escaped and were hiding in a barn at La Detrouse (143862). One of the officers was an infantryman, 2nd Lt. John Bowley (uncertain of spelling). The other was a glider pilot, Flt. Officer Adrian (Buck) Carson.

I went with a French woman and a girl to the farmhouse where the officers were hiding. On the way to the barn, we were walking down a little path through a garden, and we ran smack into two German soldiers who were digging potatoes. The woman and the girl were leading the way and had taken the wrong path which was taking us into a dead end against a wall. The two Germans were just a few feet away when the woman turned to me and asked in French where the path was. My French was so bad that I was afraid we'd be done for if I tried to answer her. But just then I saw the right path and remembered some of the little French I had learned. I just said, "Ici," and pointed to the right way. Those two Germans looked at me suspiciously, but they let us pass without saying anything.

When I reached the barn, the two French women left me, and I put a ladder up to the haymow, climbed in, and pulled the ladder up after me. The two American officers told me they had both been captured and were being taken in a truck past La Detrouse when the road was strafed by our P-51s. The truck was hit during the strafing and immobilized.

Bowley and Carson told me that a German officer ordered them shot when the truck was hit. But one German guard took the officers to some Frenchmen and gave them instructions to hide the

Kenneth Hougard with Generals Dwight Eisenhower and Omar Bradley. (Courtesy of the Laubenstein Family.)

Evade and Escape

Americans. This German guard said he would go back and tell the German officer that he had shot the two American officers. The infantry officer told me that the Frenchmen had hidden them in the haymow. They were waiting there until they would be overrun by the American troops.

I stayed in the barn with the two officers for four days. The first day a French woman brought us some milk, but the next day we didn't get any food because there were so many Germans about. We finally got so hungry that I decided to risk getting some food. I climbed out of the barn and got some peas, onions and lettuce from the garden. We made a meal out of that along with some old bread I had with me.

On 3 July, Carson, the glider pilot, came down with a fever, and he looked like he was pretty sick. The infantry officer was also suffering from his grenade wound, and he told me we couldn't stay there much longer without better food. I decided to take another chance and went to a farmhouse where I got three bottles of milk, a half bottle of whisky, potatoes, peas and a little meat from a Frenchman. We drank all the milk and ate the potatoes and peas but saved the meat for the next day. The glider pilot didn't get any better, and I was afraid we'd have to get some care for him.

I left the barn again and went to a farm where I tried to get some help from another Frenchmen. He was afraid to help us because there were so many Germans near. He kept saying: "American be here in morning. Be courageous."

I went back to the barn then and stayed there the rest of the day with the two officers. That night we could hear the Germans coming into the lower part of the barn to take some motorcycles they had stored there. But we could also hear the American guns firing and knew that our troops were getting close. Boy, we were afraid we'd get caught by the Jerries just at the last moment.

On the morning of July 4 our artillery began laying down a barrage on a hill just east of the barn. We just lay there in the hay, keeping quiet, and listening for American voices. When we finally did hear some voices, we couldn't make out whether they were German or American. Then at last we heard someone say: "Bring a squad of men and search the house!" We knew then that those were our infantry.

Lt. Bowley and I were watching through the window and saw four or five Americans going down the road past the barn. One of them stopped for a moment, and Lt. Bowley stuck his head out the window and yelled, "Hey, soldier! Stand there and don't let anyone shoot at us. We're Americans!"

A lieutenant from the 79th Division (?) came up then and arranged to send the two officers to the hospital for first aid and to send me back to the rear.

We first had breakfast with a Frenchman at a farmhouse. Those Frenchmen were certainly glad to see the American troops. They crowded around, shook hands with everyone, and kissed them. They were happy as heck!

It seems poetically fitting that Kenneth Hougard and his fellow soldiers were finally rescued by the Americans in the Allied advance on the Fourth of July...Independence Day. Kenneth Hougard would be headed home.

[If a man was able to Evade and Escape, and somehow make his way back to his unit, his war was over. The Allies couldn't risk sending a man back into combat once he obtained intimate knowledge of the Underground Resistance and their methods. If that man was captured a second time, it could jeopardize the lives of many good people.]

Conclusion

The legacy of the 384th Bombardier Group is one of sacrifice, heroism, loss, dedication and eventual victory. For many of the men who came home, the loss of so many good men weighed on them very heavily, often outweighing the satisfaction of completing the job they were trained to do. They lost men with whom they had become very close, through training, living, and fighting together. They lost friends. They lost men who they commanded in battle. And they invariably, inevitably lost some of themselves. How could they not?

Most people, thankfully and mercifully, have never had to experience the trauma and horror of witnessing the violent loss of a loved one in the heat of battle. Most people have not had to struggle to find a way to cope with the constant, sudden erasure of people from their lives because they didn't return from the latest mission, knowing all along that they could have been the one who didn't return…or who wouldn't return from the next mission.

It's been over eighty years since the B-17s of Herbert Small, Earl Allison and Joseph Cittadini went down. There were many others from the 384th lost, as well. Most of the men who survived those times are gone now, finally reunited with their long-lost comrades in arms. There aren't many of the Greatest Generation left, which is part of the reason telling these stories and talking about these men is so important and needs to continue. Without these men, and the sacrifices they made, the United States — and indeed the world -- would likely be a very different place today.

The men of the 384th Bombardment Group, as part of the Eighth Air Force, made a tangible and very valuable contribution to the battle for victory in Europe. The bombing campaign in Europe helped to substantially shorten the war and helped to make possible the success of the D-Day invasion of Hitler's Fortress Europe. In *As Briefed*, Walter Owen's relates a note about the effectiveness of the Eighth's bombing in February of 1944 from an unnamed Intelligence Officer at Grafton-Underwood: "While this series of February attacks did not completely stop German fighter production, it did reduce production of single engine fighters [by] five-hundred and sixty or six hundred a month...It destroyed over a thousand aircraft on the ground and in the air...ball bearing production fell off sixty percent...now a definite ball bearing shortage exists."

Each enemy plane that was destroyed on the ground or in the air was another weapon removed from the fight, and the pilots shot down from the air were not easily replaced, especially later in the war. Airfields whose runways were pocked with bomb craters could not send Luftwaffe fighters into the air and had to spend their time repairing fields and machinery. And when the planes and weapons, or the factories and assembly plants that made them, were damaged or destroyed, it made it increasingly more difficult for Germany to carry on the war effort.

The Eighth Air Force had so reduced the aircraft production abilities of Germany, as well as the Luftwaffe's ability to operate as a whole, that on D-Day, the skies over Normandy were virtually free of enemy aircraft. The Allies owned the skies over Normandy, and the Luftwaffe played almost no part in the defenses on D-Day. This alone saved countless lives at the landing beaches, where soldiers pinned down on the beach — especially at Omaha Beach — may have been slaughtered by the thousands had Luftwaffe fighters been in the air to strafe their ranks.

1st Lt. Herbert W. Small — like so many other brave young men

Conclusion

of his era — played a very small part in what the Eighth Air Force was able to accomplish. He wasn't necessarily unique, and if he were here today, he would undoubtedly reject the notion that he was a hero, as so many of them did. Even if none of those men consider themselves heroes, most of the Free World would probably argue otherwise. They are heroes to us. Without the fighting men in the air, on the ground, in the foxholes and on the high seas, we would live in a very different world right now.

Herb's story was cut short by war, some would say in the prime of his life, but I would argue that at age twenty-three, he was nowhere near his prime. Had fate not had other plans, I think he would have gone on to do even greater things after the war. He left an impact on many others, even after so brief a time in the world. He and the other men he died with will never know how they touched the lives of so many others; their families, friends, fellow airmen and even those who knew them only as the "Americans in the Air" over France.

Sometimes overlooked in these stories of the bombers are the people who were on the ground, in France in particular, enduring first the occupation by the Germans, and then the necessary but awful experience of the bombing from the Allies. The Americans made a strong effort to minimize collateral damage to property and lives, but there certainly was plenty of both. Despite that harsh reality, the humble and grateful residents of Normandy were often outspoken in their gratitude.

In my Aunt Cece's (Herb's sister) records were copies of some correspondence between a French woman named Madeleine Levaslot, who was a resident of Cherbourg, and the parents of S/Sgt. David E. George (One of the men who died with Herb.) Madame Levaslot was not a witness to the B-17 crash that claimed the lives of Herbert Small and his crew, but was described by a priest at St. Clements Church in Cherbourg named E.M. Guyard as "…a person who devoted herself heartily to the American soldier's cause."

Those words from Pere Guyard were part of a short note he wrote, to be included with Madeleine's letter of November 30th, 1945 to the parents of S/Sgt. George. Her letter, included here in its entirety,

Bombs Away

illustrates how the people of Normandy felt during those dark days:
Dear Mr. And Mrs. George:

>Mrs. Lerner will give you every detail concerning your dear son, but we would only express to you our deepest feeling of sympathy and respect.
>
>We lost our mother during the tragic days, and we know too well how useless it is to try to bring any consolation by words, even if they are said with the best of ourselves.
>
>But we would like you to know how sincerely we share your great pain and how we thought of you all parents of American boys when the planes of your boys attacked and [were]shot down by the Jerries' guns.
>
>If you knew with what anxiety we were watching them when they were coming to bomb us; we knew the Jerries had a wonderful gunner who every day was shooting down at least three or more planes.
>
>Very often the A.A.F. were bringing us ruin, desolation, and death, but they could not help it and we knew we should have to pay a heavy price to be freed and to get rid of the Jerry — but your boys were so simply brave and courageous, they had to go through so many dangers themselves that we could only admire and love them and pray for them.
>
>If this may be a consolation, do remember that your courageous son and his companions did not go alone to their last resting place; they were honored by the French people, in spite of the Jerries, and accompanied by our loving admiration and respectful presences. Their graves have always been flowered and we shall never forget that it's thanks to the sacrifices of so many of your courageous boys that we have been freed from misery and moral corruption coming from the German invad-

Conclusion

ers.

    Be proud of your son, Dear Mr. And Mrs. George, he — as well as his comrades — was a hero. They personified courage itself and our eyes were not large enough to follow them in the sky. We may say that many faces of men and women were covered with tears when their plane was shot down. I don't think they have suffered; it was too quickly down.

    Be blessed, dear parents of one of those boys who were bringing us every hope of freedom and liberty in the dark days of occupation.

    Be blessed and believe in our affection.

Madeleine, Jeanne and Suzanne Levaslot

-- Could we keep the snaps of David and friends as a souvenir? I shall know very soon the number of his grave in Blosville and as soon as we have means of transportation, we shall go then to take a picture of the graves if it may help.

Madeleine.

    This letter from the Levaslots confirms that the loss of these American lives was not only felt by those at home in the States or by those whom they fought alongside...their loss was also felt deeply and mourned by those for whom they were fighting. American visitors to France may not always feel this spirit from the residents of Paris or the French Riviera, but I can personally attest to there still being a palpable friendship and appreciation from many who reside in Normandy...in particular those who have the deep roots of many generations in the region. They have no doubt been told the stories, just as I was told of my Uncle Herb, of the brave men who selflessly helped to free them from the

Bombs Away

brutal occupation of the Germans.

So much of the Normandy region still bears the scars, now faded but still visible, of the tremendous battles that raged throughout the area. Bullet marks pock the masonry of centuries-old buildings, the earth itself holds bomb craters that have never been filled in and the region is filled with memorials and monuments that commemorate the battles and remind us to never forget. The region seems to wear its scars as a painful yet proud reminder of what it endured.

Herbert Small lived a little less than twenty-four years, and up until August of 2023 and March of 2024 respectively, his last surviving "kid sisters" Cece and Mary were still talking about him with love and loss. He left an indelible mark on the hearts of everyone who knew him, and on the hearts of everyone who learned about him from those who knew and loved him.

I was born twenty-eight years after he was killed on his 27th mission over Europe. I never got the chance to know him. I only knew of him from the lovingly told stories and references made by my family. Until I visited his gravesite at the American Cemetery in Normandy, he was just another long-lost relative who had fought in a war a long time ago. I didn't understand at first why that moment made such an emotional impression on me.

Upon reflection in the weeks and months that followed that visit to the cemetery, I realized that I was emotional because at that moment, the war had gone from being academic to personal; it had gone from a thing of books and movies to a tangible reality. It was no longer a distant war that was fought by millions of anonymous soldiers; instead it had a real connection to my family.

I cried at the grave of my great-uncle because he had just become a real person to me; a real twenty-three-year-old "kid," who was more of a man than most now will ever be, taken from this world much too early. He had volunteered to fight an enemy he did not know, on behalf of 125 million Americans he had never met, in defense of ideals that most people now take for granted. I feel certain he did not take them for granted.

Conclusion

He came from Sheffield, the same small town where I grew up; he lived in a house that until recently still belonged to our family where I had also lived for a while; he traveled to a foreign land and fought and died far away from home. He came from humble beginnings and made a difference in the effort to preserve our liberty, and he left literal marks on the world in the form of the monuments to him and his crew, as well as the grave that marks his final resting place.

The death of Herbert Small left a hole in his family that was felt strongly at the time and is still felt today. His mother Cecelia -- known to most of her descendants as "Nanny," his sisters Mary, Ann and Cece, and his brother Jim all felt his loss profoundly. His brother Jim, my grandfather, also fought in the air during World War II, as a bombardier on B-29s in the Pacific, a world away from his younger brother. For years, Lt. Col. James G. Small led the annual Memorial Day parade as the highest-ranking military officer in Sheffield, at least partly in proud tribute to his lost brother.

Herb is memorialized in three countries and on two continents; in his hometown of Sheffield, in the town of Bricquebec, France, and at the American Cemetery in Normandy in France, and finally at Saint Paul's Cathedral in London, where he is listed in a special book of American military Killed in Action during World War II..

I'm very glad to have known my grandfather and his three sisters, two of whom have only left us recently, but I feel like I missed out on something special having never gotten the chance to know my great-uncle Herb. When I started this project, I saw a picture of him for the first time; he was in his uniform for his flight school yearbook. To me, he looked very much like my grandfather and his siblings, all of whom I had known very well in my life…so perhaps I did know him in a 'Small' way after all.

H. W. Small

Bibliography

Websites

303rd BG (H). (1944). Mission 111 - 1. http://www.303rdbg.com/missionreports/111/pdf

303rd BG (H). B-17 *Crewmen duties and responsibilities*. (n.d.). http://www.303rdbg.com/crew-duties.html

384thBombGroup.com, Grafton Underwood Airfield, AAF Station 106. (n.d.). https://www.384thbombgroup.com/_content/_pages/gu.php

B-17G. *Equipment, turbo-superchargers*. (n.d.). https://airpages.ru/eng/mn/b17_18.shtml

Collection: Joseph L. Cittadini collection. Florida State University ArchivesSpace. (n.d.). https://archives.lib.fsu.edu/repositories/10/resources/918tr

Grafton Underwood. American Air Museum in Britain. https://www.americanairmuseum.com/archive/place/Grafton-underwood

1LT Jack Cameron "Big Foot" Nagel (1920-1944) -... (1920, June 25). https://www.findagrave.com/memorial/114491406/jack-cameron-nagel

Kylie, N. (2023, November 24). *Everything you need to know about the 'Flying Fortress' B-17 bomber.* Simple Flying. https://simpleflying.com/b-17-bomber-flying-fortress-guide/

Maschino, J. (2021, August 23). *Eagle Archives, Aug. 23, 1952: Sheffield's 115-year-old covered bridge may be purchased for the sum of only $1.* The Berkshire Eagle.com/history/eagle-archives-aug-23-1952-

sheffields-115-year-old-covered-bridge-may-be-purchased-for/article_d53daae4-011e-11ec-8b1b-7348c07df4ae.html

National Museum of the Mighty Eighth Air Force. (2024, February 22). *Brief History of the Eighth Air Force | National Museum of the Mighty 8th Air Force.* https://www.mightyeighth.org/brief-history-of-the-eighth-air-force/

Petersen, J. (2023, March 17). *World War II - Historic Wendover Airfield.* Historic Wendover Airfield. https://wendoverairfield.org/world-war-2/

Smithsonian Magazine. (2007, March 1). *In the Footsteps of the Mighty Eighth.* Smithsonian.com. https://www.smithsonianmag.com/air-space-magazine/in-the-footsteps-of-the-mighty-eighth-15806031/

Stalag Luft POW camps for Airmen during WWII. (n.d.). The 392nd Bomb Group. https://b24.net/powCamps.htm

Paula Stewart. (2022, April 16). *Detailed tour through a Boeing B-17 Flying Fortress (as featured on Masters of the Air) [Video].* YouTube. https://youtube.com/watch?v=h4_ESnENDfl

The guns of the B-17 Flying Fortress (n.d.). Guns.com. https://www.guns.com/news/2024/01/19/the-guns-of-the-b-17-flying-fortress

The mighty Eighth calendar. (n.d.). HTTPS://www.scottylive.com/mac_calendar/1943/Dec1943.html

Two world wars made molybdenum famous — refractory molybdenum. (n.d.). Http://molybdenum42.com/two-world-wars-made-molybdenum-famous/

V1 launch sites - TracesOfWar.com. (n.d.). HTTPS://www.tracesofwar.

Bibliography

com/themes/4437/V1-launchsites.htm?show=map

Wikipedia. *Army Air Forces Training Command.* Retrieved January 9, 2024 from https://en.wikipedia.org/wiki Army_Air_Forces_ Training_ Command#References

Wikipedia contributors. (2024, February 28). *V-1 flying bomb facilities.* Wikipedia. https://en.wikipedia.org/wiki/V-1_flying_bomb-facilities

Wikipedia contributors. (2024, February 29). *Aggie Yell Leaders.* Wikipedia. https://en.wikipedia.org/wiki/Aggie_Yell_Leaders

Wikipedia contributors. (2024, June 5). *Combat box.* Wikipedia. https://en.wikipedia.org/wiki/Combat_box

WWII Prisoners of War. (n.d.). National Museum of the United States Air Force. https://www.nationalmuseum.af.mil/Visit/Museum-Exhibits/Fact- Sheets/Display/Article/196125/wwii-prisoners-of-war/

Books

Astor, Gerald. (1997). *The Mighty Eighth: The Air War in Europe as Told by the Men Who Fought It.* Donald I. Fine Books.

Bowman, Martin W. (1984) *Castles in the Air: The Story of the B-17 Flying Fortress crews of the US 8th Air Force.* Stephens.

Bowman, Martin W. (2017). *Clash of Eagles: USAAF 8th Air Force Bombers versus the Luftwaffe in World War II.* Pen and Sword Aviation.

Cittadini, J. L. (2006). *20th Mission: A short account as well as my memory serves.* Unpublished.

Darling, I. (2016). *Heroes in the skies: American Aviators in World War II.* Sterling.

Freeman, Roger A. (1984). *The Might Eighth War Manual*. Jane's Publishing Company.

Kaplan, P. & Smith, R.A. (1983). *One Last Look: A Sentimental Journey to the Eighth Air Force Heavy Bomber Bases of World War II in England*. Abbeville Press Publishers.

Kaufman, Vernon H. (n.d.). *"Our Career" of "Little Barney."* Unpublished War Diary.

Keyshawn, A. (2005). *The Longest Winter: The Battle of the Bulge and the Epic Story of World War II's Most Decorated Platoon*. Da Capo Press.

Laubenstein, William F. *A Quiet Hero: The true story of a WWII POW.* (Unpublished).

McAloon, G. (n.d.) *A personal tribute to: Scott A. Bailey, 384th Bomb Group Pilot.* (Unpublished)

McCrary, John R. and Sherman, David E. (1944) *First of the Many, A Journal of Action with the Men of the Eighth Air Force*. Simon and Schuster.

McLaughlin, Brig. Gen. J. Kemp. (2000). *The Mighty Eighth in WWII: A Memoir*. The University Press of Kentucky.

Nordyke, Phil. (2005). *All American All the Way: The Combat History of the 82nd Airborne Division in World War II*. Zenith Press.

Overy, R. J. (2014). *The bombers and the bombed: Allied Air War Over Europe 1940-1945*. Viking Adult.

Owens, Capt. Walter E. (1946). *As Briefed: a family history of the*

Bibliography

384th Bombardment Group.

Sisson, F. (2020). *I Marched With Patton: A Firsthand Account of World War II Alongside one of the U.S. Army's Greatest Generals.* William Morrow, Harper Collins Publishers.

Smith, Major Gen. Dale O. (1990). *Screaming Eagle: Memoirs of a B-17 Group Commander.* Dell Publishing.

Smith, S. (2006). *Jimmy Stewart: Bomber Pilot.* Zenith Press.

Snyder, S. (2015). *Shot Down: The true story of pilot Howard Snyder and the crew of the B-17 Susan Ruth.* Sea Breeze Publishing.

United States Army Air Forces. (1944). *Target: Germany - The U.S. Army Air Forces' official story of the VIII Bomber Command's first year over Europe.* His Majesty's Stationery Office.

Wilson, K. (2017). *Blood and fears: How America's Bomber Boys of the 8th Air Force Saved World War II.* Pegasus Books.

Zaloga, S. (2011). *Operation Pointblank 1944: Defeating the Luftwaffe.* Osprey Publishing.

Newspaper Articles

In memory of the Mighty 8th. (1977, September 26). Evening Telegraph.

Movies

Nelson, Erik, director. The Cold Blue. Kino Lorber, 2020.

Bombs Away

Acknowledgements and Thanks

The process of doing this project has been one of the most rewarding experiences of my life. I have met and interacted with some of the most generous, kind and helpful people I ever could have imagined. At each turn, every person that I reached out – from family members of 384th Bomber Group personnel, to World War II enthusiasts, to historians…and everyone in between – has been incredibly willing to help with information, encouragement and advice.

I only hope that in expressing my thanks, I don't overlook anyone.

Among the most instrumental to the success of this project -- or at least the completion -- was the incredible fountain of 384th Bombardment Group knowledge that is **www.384thBombGroup.com**, and those that run it and administer the site. In particular, Christopher Wilkinson, Keith Ellefson and Fred Preller were incredibly helpful.

There are many others to thank:

- Paul Teal and Sam Coleman of the Facebook page **RAF Grafton-Underwood's WW2 Memories**.
- Keith Andrews of the **384th Bombardment Group Museum** Facebook page.
- Mikayla Leech, author of an incredible collection of 384th pictures and information related to her grandfather 2nd Lt. R.O. Henley, a pilot in the 384th, titled *From Stephenville, Texas to Stalag Luft 3*.

- Several of my family members and friends have helped me great-

ly, including:
   - Mary Ustico, Cecelia Kay, Stanley Kay, Ann Detlefs, Maureen Seward, Sheila Smith and Craig Delehanty.

- Several family members of the men who flew with Herbert Small, including:
   - Mrs. Donna (Kaufman) Wiley, sister of Vernon Kaufman.
   - Erin Dowd, niece of William Laubenstein, and her husband Jake.
   - Richard Laubenstein, son of William Laubenstein.
   - Peter Hougard, grandson of Kenneth Hougard.

- Steve Snyder, author of the wonderful book Shot Down.
- Paul O'Brien and James Miller at the Sheffield Historical Society.
- My wife Jennifer Schroer for proofreading, edits and putting up with my obsession for the last eighteen months.

Special Note Regarding Rank

Regarding the various military personnel named and described in this book, I have endeavored to be as accurate as I could with each man's rank. However, rank was often changing due to promotion or demotion; Sergeants became Staff or Tech Sergeants...or Privates, sometimes. 2nd Lieutenants became 1st Lieutenants; Captains became Majors or Colonels. I tried to list each man's rank in accordance to what moment the reference to that man occurred, such that it was accurate to that time. If the man was a 2nd Lieutenant when the event(s) occurred, I listed him as such, even if he later became a 1st Lieutenant or higher. Please forgive any errors, and if you find some, please inform me and I can correct in future editions.

Index

Symbols

1st Bomb Division 125
15th Bomber Squadron 45
41st Combat Wing 125, 131, 153
97th Bomber Group 45
100th Bomb Group 101
303rd Bomber Group 131, 150
305th Bomb Group 45
379th Bomber Group 131
384th Bombardment Group 39, 41, 45, 51, 55, 137, 153, 166, 177, 209, 237-238
388th Bomb Group 150
544th Bomber Squadron 41

A

Alconbury, UK 42
Allio, 2nd Lt. Orion R. 167, 171
Allison, 2nd Lt. Earl T. 39, 95, 98, 100-102, 106-108, 110-111, 116, 132, 133-135, 139, 142, 144-146, 152-161, 166-167, 169-171, 173-176, 178-181, 190, 192, 211-213, 225
American Cemetery in Normandy 1, 4, 21, 172, 182, 230-231
April's Fool 206
Army Air Force 24, 32, 33, 41, 43, 44, 89, 95, 103, 110, 111

B

B-24 Liberator 31, 151
B-25 Mitchell (medium bomber) 31
Bailey, 2nd Lt. William E. 108, 148, 150, 175, 236
Sperry Ball Turret
  Ball Turret 70, 76
Ball Turret Gunner 77, 96, 100, 112-113, 133, 165, 167, 179-180, 195, 211
Bassingbourn, UK 42
Berkshire County, Massachusetts 7, 9, 18
Berlin First 94, 152, 154, 158, 159
Beverly, Massachusetts 100, 114
Bier, S/Sgt. Irvin L. 195, 196
Big Stupe 12, 79
Big Week 140, 147-149, 150-152
Billy, Reverend Method 188
Black Thursday 117, 119

Index

Boeing B-17 Flying Fortress 24, 30, 33, 41, 45, 50, 54, 55, 69, 70, 71-77, 80, 83, 87, 89-90, 100, 102, 103, 106-107, 109, 111, 119, 125, 126, 133, 145, 149, 151, 154, 160, 179, 181, 191, 194-195, 197, 198, 227, 233, 234-235, 237
Boger, 1st Lt. Eugene A. 63, 116, 132
Bombardier 80, 81, 82, 96, 100, 103, 112, 165, 167, 179, 195, 211, 225, 226
Boomerang 57, 114
Boone, Jr., Tech Sgt. James D. 180
Bricquebec, France 181, 183, 192, 231
Brown, 2nd Lt. James Jefferson 122, 196
Browning .50-caliber Machine Gun 70, 75-76, 78-79, 79, 81-83, 103, 123, 123
Bruchsal, Germany 151
Bushnell Sage library 19

C

Chelveston, UK 42
Chin Turret 79
Cittadini, 1st Lt. Joseph L.G. 108, 110-111, 115, 122-123, 155, 160-161, 163-164, 174, 177-178, 190-191, 194-198, 201-205, 207, 225, 233, 235
Clark, Staff Sgt. Alfred A. 113, 139
Clayton, 1st Lt. John E. 154
Clean Cut 77, 149
Cleland, Tech. Sgt. Deston K. 113, 135
Clements, Staff Sgt. William A. 98, 100, 104, 106, 155, 167, 179-180, 211, 213, 227
Cloud, Tech. Sgt. Doy J. 113, 116, 128, 131
Cochran, Staff Sgt. Thomas T. 180
Combat Box 83, 127
Compton, Staff Sgt. Robert L. 96, 116, 144
Corbett, Tech Sgt. Thomas W. 180
Corpening, Tech Sgt. Robert C. 180
Curtin, 1st. Lt. John Q. 63, 93, 96, 116, 166-167, 178-180, 191, 211

D

Davis, Lt. David H. 96
Deenethorpe, UK 42
DeFrees, 2nd Lt. Norman F. 149
Dolan, Lt. Col. William E. "Pop" 47
Doolittle, Lt. Gen. James "Jimmy" 140, 147
Douve River 192, 215
Drogue, Capt. Arthur J. 113, 144, 155, 157
Duke of Buccleuch 50, 51
Duro, Pvt. Victor H. 96
Dynamite Express 15, 89, 92, 139

E

East Anglia, UK 41, 42, 43
Eighth Air Force 24, 43, 44, 45, 73, 86, 118, 130, 139, 140, 141, 150, 158, 160, 234, 236
El Rauncho 18, 97, 117
Estes , UK 60
Ex-Virgin 90
Eye, UK 42

F

Fairview Hospital 23
Fallon, 2nd Lt. John J. 113
Finn, Ann (Small) 11-13, 15, 23, 35, 38, 172, 231
Finn, Joseph 38
Fisher, Staff Sgt. James J. 113, 148
Flak 24, 55, 72, 74, 87-88, 109-110, 119, 121-124, 129, 130-131, 135, 139, 143, 146, 149, 153, 160, 163-164, 167, 169, 170-171, 178, 184, 191, 195, 197, 208, 210, 212, 214
Flak House 31, 134, 156
Flight Engineer 79
Focke-Wulf 74, 87, 133
Ford, Bridget (Henaghan) 5, 20
Ford, Patrick 5, 6, 7, 9, 22
Foster, 1st Lt. James E. 154, 178-181, 183
Foxy Theatre 49, 56
Framingham, UK 42
Frazier, Tech. Sgt. Ernest L. 113
French Underground Resistance 107, 160, 175, 181, 190, 192, 194, 202, 217, 224

G

Gardner, 2nd Lt. Sam 96, 98, 100, 102-103, 132, 146, 155, 160-162, 178
Geary, 2nd Lt. James E. 174, 196
George, Staff Sgt. David E. 112-113, 165, 173, 227
Goetz, Staff Sgt. Jack K. 96, 116, 144
Goin' Dog 111, 154
Goller Jr., 2nd Lt. Theodore "Teddy" 122, 155, 161, 177, 194, 195, 196
Gorham, Sgt. Donald F. 96, 116
Grafton-Underwood Airbase 39, 42, 44-48, 50, 56-58, 63, 65-68, 86, 97, 108, 115, 117, 123, 125, 129, 133, 135, 137, 149, 160, 178, 187, 190
Great Barrington, Massachusetts 9, 23, 61
Gregori, Tech Sgt. Aldo J. 96, 116
Grilli, Flight Officer Eugene P. 195
Grimmett, Staff Sgt. James H. 98, 100, 108-109, 143, 147, 155, 167, 179, 180, 190, 192, 193, 211, 213

Index

H

Halesworth, UK 42
Hall, St. Sgt. Lawrence M. 113, 144, 149, 221
Hard to Get 90
Harper, Staff Sgt. William L. 113, 145, 151
Hausenfluck, Jr., 1st Lt. Jesse Dee 60
Healey, Allan 123
Hedouin, L'Abbe Raymond 218, 219
Hells Angels 150
Hell's Messenger 89, 161, 162
Hougard, Staff Sgt. Kenneth N. 98, 100, 106,-108, 110, 135, 139, 155, 167, 179-180, 190-192, 209-213, 221-222, 224, 239
Housatonic River 9, 14
Howell, Staff Sgt. Roy F. 113, 195, 196
Hutchison, Tech. Sgt. William W. 113

I

Idiots Delight 89

J

Jacobs, Capt. Randolph G. E. 39, 63, 96-98, 115-117, 120, 127, 129, 131-132, 144, 147, 149, 178-180, 211-212
Jeter, Jr., 2nd Lt. Sydney R. 148, 150
Jeter, June (McClure) 150
Johnson, 2nd Lt. Clifford L. 180
June Bug 148, 150

K

Kaufman, Staff Sgt. Vernon H. 98, 100, 109-110, 133, 139, 143, 146, 155, 167, 171, 179,-180, 185-186, 211, 213, 236, 239
Kay, Cecelia (Small) 10-16, 19, 23-24, 33-35, 38, 173-175, 227, 230-231
Kay, Joseph 38
Kennedy, Robert M. 60, 150
Kew, 2nd Lt. William J. 149
Kiel, Germany 139
Kline, Alice 61
Kouski, Staff Sgt. William L. 98, 100, 104, 110, 143-147, 149, 151-152

L

Lacey, Col. Julius K. "Con" 119-120
La Fiere Bridge 182
LaSalle, St. Sgt. Angelo A. 113, 146

Bombs Away

Laubenstein, Tech Sgt. William F. 35, 37, 39, 71, 98, 100-101, 103-105, 107, 109, 121, 124, 155-156, 167, 169, 179-180, 189, 190, 192, 193, 198, 200, 204, 210, 211, 212-213, 222, 236, 239
Le Foyer, France, 179
Liberty Run 144, 153
Life Magazine 152, 154, 158
Lingen, Germany 149
Little Barney 6, 35, 71, 98, 101, 133, 142, 146, 148, 151, 236
Little Willie 90
London, UK 44, 60, 61, 64, 85, 114, 143, 173, 192, 211, 217, 231
Loose Goose 48, 153
Luftwaffe 79, 82, 87, 119, 141, 145, 147, 152, 160, 226, 235, 237

M

Mae West Life Preserver 101, 124
Marienburg, Germany 157
Markow, 1st Lt. Henry V. 149
Martin, 2nd Lt. Gregory L. 195
Masters of the Air 43, 101, 234
Matican, Staff Sgt. Sigmund S. 180
McDonald, 2nd Lt. Raymond L. 149
McGue, 2nd Lt. James E. 112, 165
McKinney, 2nd Lt. David L. 113, 131
McLean Hospital Nursing School 23, 24
McMillin, Lt. Col. Selden L. 178
McNasty, Sgt. Delbert P. 58-60
Memphis Belle 89
Merced, California 26, 33
Merritt, Capt. James M. 106, 113, 133, 144
Messerschmitt-109 87, 194
Messerschmitt Me-210 194
Milk Run 108, 162, 164, 167
Molesworth, UK 42, 45, 150
Moosberg, Germany 191, 202, 204, 205
Morris, 2nd Lt. Roy J. 112, 165
Morrison, Donald S. 154
Mr. Five by Five 16, 145, 151

N

Nagel, 2nd Lt. Jack C. 98, 100, 103, 155, 156, 158, 167, 179-180, 211-213, 233
Narog, St. Sgt. John 113, 144
Navigator 80-81, 96, 100, 102, 110, 112-113, 123, 131, 155, 165, 167, 179-180, 194, 195, 211
New Marlborough, Massachusetts 9

Index

Newton, Dr. Wesley 147
Nissen Huts 45, 52
Nissen, Lt. Col. Peter N. 52
Noball Sites 135, 143
Norden Bomb Sight 81-82
Normandy, France 1, 4, 21, 107-108, 143, 160, 165, 172, 180-182, 226-227, 229-231
Northern Route 37
North Sea 124, 125, 129, 130, 133
Nose Art 89
Nuttall's Nut House 7, 89, 133, 144, 149, 157, 166, 167, 171, 172

O

Our Lady of the Valley Catholic Church 9, 14
Overcash, Jr., Staff Sgt. Jimmy L. 180
Owens, Capt. Walter E. 51, 53, 57, 86, 97, 236

P

P-38 Lightning 42, 87, 117
P-47 Thunderbolt 42, 87, 100, 117, 143, 219
P-51 Mustang 42, 72, 88, 140, 141, 147
Parker, Staff Sgt. Marion L. 112, 165, 170-171, 186
Patton, Gen. George S. 204-205, 207-208, 237
Patton's Third Army 204-205, 208
Phartzac 22, 89-90
Piccadilly Commandos 60
Pirrello, Sgt. Richard D. 112, 165
Pistol Packin' Mama 89
Polebrook, UK 42
Potkay, Sgt. Edward J. 112, 165-166
Preuseville, France 152
Purdy, Tech. Sgt. Alan B. 113, 144
Purple Heart Corner 83

R

Radio Operator 78, 96, 100, 103, 112-113, 121, 131, 165, 167, 179-180, 195
Rain of Terror 72, 89
Randie Lou 90
Rauville-la-Place, France 217, 218
Red Cross 54, 56, 60, 130, 199, 208
Reed, Staff Sgt. Clarence E. 195, 196
Regan, Sgt. Charles T. 153
Reno's Raider 89, 108, 178, 179, 190, 212
Reynolds, Sgt. John B. 112, 165, 173
Rocheville, France 21, 170, 181

Bombs Away

Ross, Staff Sergeant William J. 149
Roswell Army Flying School 34
Roswell, New Mexico 34
Royal Air Force (RAF) 44, 123, 130

S

Sagan-Silesia, Germany 191
Sanders, Major Russell A. 180
Satan's Sister 90
Schenob Brook 15
Schock, 2nd Lt. George W. 160
Schweinfurt, Germany 69, 97, 110, 116, 117, 151, 160
Screaming Eagle 64, 140
Sea Hag 14, 47, 134, 135
Sewack, 2nd Lt. John M. 112, 165, 186
Sexy Suzy 89
Shack Rabbit 10, 146, 152
Shannon, Tech. Sgt. Lucian G. 160
Sheffield High School 17, 18, 19
Shipdham, UK 64
Sioux City Army Airbase 99
Small, Cecelia (Ford) "Nanny" 5, 10-12, 20, 23, 38, 175-176, 231
Small, Janet (Eadie) 5, 7
Small, Lt. Col. James (Jim) 11-13, 16-20, 24-25, 28, 231
Small, Marion (Mulligan) 20
Small, William 5
Smith, Jr., 2nd Lt. Paul M. 149
Smith, Col. Dale O. 48, 50, 51, 55, 81, 90, 106, 113, 119-120, 134, 136, 139-140, 155-157, 178
Smith, Staff Sgt. Leland R. 113, 113, 146, 151
Snetterton Heath, UK 42
Sottevast, France 164, 178, 211
Southern Route 37
Spotted Cow 89
Stalag 13-D 111
Stalag Luft III 111, 198, 201, 207
Stalag Luft IV 109, 193, 198, 200, 204
Stalag Luft VII-A 202, 204
Stalag Luft XIII-D 204
Ste-Colombe, France 192, 214, 216-217
Ste-Mere-Eglise, France 181, 182
Ste.-Sauveur-le-Vicomte, France 217, 218, 220
Stevens, Staff Sgt. John J. 113, 147, 180
Stewart, Lt. Col. James "Jimmy" 31, 56, 61-62

Index

St.-Jacques-de-Nehou, France 192, 193
St.-Nicholas-de-Pierrepont, France 218, 219
Susan Ruth 89-91
Swanson, 2nd Lt. Kenneth J. 148, 150
Sweater Girl 90

T

Tail-End Charlie 83
Tail gunner 54, 76, 84, 106, 111, 139, 153, 157, 164, 166, 171, 179-180, 190, 209, 211, 221
Thorpe Abbots, UK 42
Thurleigh, UK 42
Top Turret 79, 96, 100, 106, 112, 113, 165, 167, 179, 195, 211
Tremblin Gremlin 105

U

Ulrey, 2nd Lt. Edgar E. 134
Ulrich, Sgt. Russell H. 112, 165, 250
Uniszkiewicz, 2nd Lt. Joseph K. 180
Ursta, Staff Sgt. George 113, 148, 250

V

V-1 Rocket 135, 143, 152, 154, 178
Vertical Shaft 42, 90
Virgin on the Verge 89
Visalia-Dinuba School of Aeronautics 33, 35
Vultee BT-13 Valiant 30, 31

W

Wabbit Twacks 17, 178, 180
Wager, Staff Sgt. Lawrence H. 96-97, 147, 250
Waist Gunner 96, 106, 110, 180, 195, 211
Walton, Sgt. Horace M. 195
Watts, 1st Lt. Lowell H.
Way, Sgt. Arthur H. 195-196, 250
Wearne, Staff Sgt. Walter E. 195
Wendover Airfield 100, 234
West, 1st Lt. George B. 154
Wormingford, UK 42

Y

Yankee Lady 89